January 2006

To Dear Evelyn —
with
fondest regards,

"Margy"

My Darling Margy
The World War II Diaries and Letters
of Surgeon Charles Francis Chunn, MD

©2005 The Scuppernong Press
The Scuppernong Press
an Imprint of Sojourner Publishing, Inc.
Wake Forest, NC USA

The Scuppernong Press: www.thescuppernongpress.com
First trade paperback edition
Manufactured in the United States of America

Library of Congress Control Number: 2005933345

International Standard Book Number (ISBN) 0-9773156-0-6

My Darling Margy

The World War II Diaries and
Letters of Surgeon
Charles Francis Chunn, MD

Edited by Celeste Chunn Colcord

The Scuppernong Press
Wake Forest, NC

We all believe that this work is dedicated
by the author
to the love of his life,
Marjorie Wright Moore Chunn

My Darling Margy

If

If you can keep your head when all about you
Are losing theirs and blaming it on you;
If you can trust yourself when all men doubt you,
But make allowance for their doubting too;
If you can wait and not be tired by waiting,
Or being lied about, don't deal in lies,
Or being hated, don't give way to hating,
And yet don't look too good, nor talk too wise:

If you can dream — and not make dreams your master;
If you can think — and not make thoughts your aim;
If you can meet with Triumph and Disaster
And treat those two imposters just the same;
If you can bear to hear the truth you've spoken
Twisted by knaves to make a trap for fools,
Or watch the things you gave your life to, broken,
And stoop and build 'em up with worn-out tools;

If you can make one heap of all your winnings
And risk it on one turn of pitch-and-toss,
And lose, and start again at your beginnings
And never breathe a word about your loss;
If you can force your heart and nerve and sinew
To serve your turn long after they are gone,
And so hold on when there is nothing in you
Except the Will which says to them: "Hold on!"

If you can talk with crowds and keep your virtue,
Or walk with kings — nor lose the common touch,
If neither foes nor loving friends can hurt you,
If all men count with you, but none too much;
If you can fill the unforgiving minute
With sixty seconds' worth of distance run —
Yours is the Earth and everything that's in it,
And — which is more — you'll be a Man, my son!

From *Rewards and Fairies* by Rudyard Kipling, copyright 1910

My Darling Margy

Major C—

"There is nothing unusual about the operating room. In fact, it is just a tent with a board floor. There are no green or blue tiled walls, no chromium or monel metal fixtures. Light comes from ordinary bulbs backed by shiny ration tins."

Then my notes focus on the surgeon. " Major C— (I shall omit his name because it would cause him acute embarrassment to be singled out among dozens of his colleagues who are doing similar things) is thirty-two years of age, graduated from a medical school just ten years ago." The steps of his training are then reviewed: internship in a university hospital followed by a residency in another. Then a single year as assistant to a surgeon in practice in a small city. Certified by the American Board of Surgery in 1942, and a month later commissioned in the Army of the United States with overseas assignment. "Here, then," my notes continue, "is a master craftsman at the age of 32, actually performing technical procedures at the level of the Mayos, Cushing, Crile and other figures of the immediate past, and far beyond the legendary figures of Warren, Gross and Senn."
Without laboring the point, it is my personal opinion that just as thoracic surgery emerged from the first World War, so the brilliant flowering of open heart surgery which has taken place in the past two decades, both in the United States and England, can be traced, at least in part, to the changed approach to the problems of the severely wounded in World War II. Neither the magnitude of an undertaking nor the precarious condition of the patient offers an insurmountable barrier against which a well prepared surgical team can refuse to contend. I hasten to add that World War II was an experience of the entire surgical community, not only of the surgeons who participated directly by operating under canvas.

Edward D. Churchill, M.D.
Advances in Modern Surgery and Pathways to Future Progress
Rhode Island Medical Journal,
February, 1964, p.73

My Darling Margy

The World War II Diaries and Letters
of Surgeon Charles Francis Chunn, MD

Edited by Celeste Chunn Colcord

My Darling Margy

Introduction

Celeste Chunn Colcord

This wartime diary and letters were written by my father, Charles Francis Chunn. He attended Duke University, graduating from medical school in 1936. He trained as a surgeon at Henry Ford Hospital in Detroit and received a Master's in surgery in August 1940. He then did a surgical fellowship in Vicksburg, Mississippi. When all licensed and qualified to open a private practice, he and my mother moved to Tampa, Florida. The office space, equipment and staff (my mother) were ready for business in October, 1941. Just weeks later, the U.S. declared war. He volunteered for the Army on December 8, 1941. He made arrangements to finish his surgical boards, leased his equipment to another physician and the surgical practice was closed by May, 1942.

Off he went, age 29, to Camp Polk, Louisiana. On the day that this fully board-certified surgeon signed in, it was instead the internal medicine service's day to get a doctor. He was disappointed that he wouldn't be using his surgical skills but he saluted the flag and went to work. The Armored Division stationed at Camp Polk had been inoculated against yellow fever and many of the troops had come down with infectious hepatitis with several deaths as a result. He became interested in these cases and worked with them intensely. The cases and the doctor garnered the attention of the Surgeon General who sent a consultant to Camp Polk. The consultant just happened to tell Captain Chunn about a new group of well-trained surgeons that were forming the Second Auxiliary Surgical Group, a new format for the Army. The hepatitis work was important, but Captain Chunn wanted action. He was accepted by the "2nd Aux" and went to Atlanta for a period of intense physical training, horseback riding, more inoculations, pitching hospital-size tents, and evenings in the Officer's Club or the Dogwood Room of the Henry Grady Hotel. They trained for four months, an eternity to these young eager-beavers and prima donnas. Finally their teams were assigned. Each consisted of the head surgeon and an assistant, an anesthesiologist, a nurse and two or three corpsmen. They were alerted for movement in January 1943. Families were sent packing and the teams were kept secluded. They were transported to Camp Kilmer, NJ, for embarkation. My mother got one last, hurried phone call. He still didn't know where he was going.

The adventure starts in February, 1943. They sailed on a British luxury liner converted for troop transport. The H.M.S. *Andes* was very fast and traveled unescorted. He was overseas 31 months. During this time he participated in the Tunisian, Naples-Foggia, Rome-Arno, Southern France and Germany Campaigns and was authorized to wear seven Bronze Service Stars for these campaigns. He was decorated with the Silver Star, Purple Heart, European African Middle East Theater Ribbon and the American Theater Meritorious Service Plaque.

Sixty-two years after my father began writing a diary of his World War II experience my family is presenting it in published form. We want to share both the first person war experience of C. Frank Chunn and the story of a man's life that we treasure. His letters and V-Mails sent to my mother during that time have been mingled with the diary entries. The concurrent reports are repetitive in some cases but his different voices are also enlightening. The letters have more intimacy, but because of U.S. government censors, the diaries have more detail. His voices can be terse and secretive, but also loving, adventurous and devastatingly descriptive. We chose to add our voices to complete the narrative, to honor an extraordinary life and to share great moments in a family's history.

I have learned a lot about my father from his diaries. What I know of him before that time, and after, are only memories kept alive by my family. I remember a robust man who was a consummate healer. I made Sunday morning rounds and house calls with him. When holding his hand I saw the scar but never knew it was a war wound, or a "penetrating mortar fragment wound of the right hand" as the official report states.

For whatever reason you are reading this— as family or friend, surgeon, soldier or someone with a few hours to spend in another time and place, I hope there is something important for you in the pages. The foreign battlefield is a life changing event for those who experience it. Times of tedium, great adventure and challenge, terror, physical and mental exhaustion, disbelief and other very personal emotions are experienced in a place that is unfamiliar and unfriendly. Many of us will never have this kind of intense experience, but we can see from a first person account how others endure.

Only as an adult have I read these diaries, and I read them over and over. It's what our family has left to glimpse a remarkable man during extraordinary times. They are actually three small, worn notebooks of different shapes. They were hand-carried by unknown pilots, patients and comrades returning to the United States. My mother received them by mail. The words are cryptic at times. I believe some details, locations and unit names, were omitted for security concerns. And, Margy is my mother, Marjorie Moore Chunn.

My Darling Margy

Before the War

Marjorie Moore Chunn Cochran

Frank Chunn was born wanting to be a surgeon, and he was encouraged by everyone. His family was cooperative and supportive. Above all, his paternal grandmother, Clorinda D'Aubert Chunn, seemed to have had the most influence. In the apple orchard behind his home in Asheville, North Carolina, Frank had a small laboratory, well equipped with beakers, burners, and test tubes, where he spent free time during high school on chemistry experiments, and operated on rats, rabbits, and squirrels. Frank was a well-rounded youth, enjoying sports, scouts, and church activities. His dad taught him to love hunting, fishing, and gave him an appreciation of guns.

Immediately after graduating from Lee Edwards High, he went off to Duke University, and studied premed, year round, with summer schools at the University of North Carolina at Chapel Hill. After three years, he was admitted to the medical school of Duke, from which he graduated at the age of 22. He served a surgical internship and assistant residency at Duke Medical Center.

Frank would set his goal and then pursue it. His friends said he had seen a student nurse whom he said he would marry. He would meet her after taking the national board examinations. I was that student nurse.

One day he and Dr. Query came on the ward where I was working and we met. He persuaded me to go out with him that very night. We had a good time, but I thought he was presumptive, and besides, I had a boyfriend at Annapolis. Frank was so handsome and so cute that soon I was seeing him whenever we had time. He would ask for me to assist him in changing his patients' dressings, and then paint my initials in gentian violet under the dressings. When my Annapolis beau came to visit me wearing his white uniform, the interns teased Frank, singing "Anchors Aweigh" as he entered the dining hall.

My vacation was late August, and Frank made money to go to Tampa with me by selling his blood and his microscope. With his railroad pass he visited me and my parents. (As an intern, his salary was $10 a month, enough to pay for cigarettes. His room, board, and intern quarters were furnished.)

We talked to my parents, and with their blessing, planned to get married during Christmas holidays. We took the train back to Durham on the 11th of September. On the 12th, we got off the train and decided to get married in Raleigh. Our taxi driver took us to buy a license, a ring, flowers, and then to the Edenton Street Methodist Church. The taxi driver asked to stay with us, and became an official witness, along with Rev. Few and his secretary. We registered at the Sir Walter Hotel, where we had a festive brunch and spent the day, reporting to Duke for the midnight deadline. We had to keep our marriage a secret.

I didn't like the dual life and resigned from Duke Nursing School. I went home to Tampa to tell my parents. They recovered from the shock and were always supportive.

After medical school, we moved to Henry Ford Hospital in Detroit, where the resident staff were paid minimum wage and were not required to live in intern's quarters. It was a teaching hospital known for its surgical training program. During our four year stay, Frank trained me to do laboratory work, and I worked for a cardiologist in the Fischer Building. A special treat was a two-week cruise of the Great Lakes and Georgian Bay, with ports of Chicago and Mackinac Island, Midland, Ontario, and Cleveland. Frank was the ship's surgeon, and the most serious illness was my sea sickness.

Frank did research on shock and alimentary azotemia. I would walk to the lab with him during the night to help out. The experimental dogs cooperated by holding perfectly still as he took blood specimens. He always loved dogs.

After two years we saved enough to buy a second hand Ford for $150, and a used 8mm movie camera. The camera got us invited to all the residents' kids' birthday parties. There were lots of babies, and parents strapped to make ends meet, so we decided to postpone having a child until we could better afford a family. The Ford made two trips to Tampa and many trips to Ann Arbor where Frank drove every week to get his Masters in Surgery at the University of Michigan in 1940.

Other new experiences in Detroit were ice skating, ice sailing, and fishing through the ice. There were always close friends, not all of whom were poor. We even had a Duke heiress who was married to a Ford Hospital intern. There was time for the symphony, conducted by Eugene Ormandy then, and the art museum for the French Impressionists.

Frank was impressed with the training he was getting at Ford, which did the most hernias and industrial accidents of any hospital. He was even called to Henry Ford's home on a Sunday afternoon to sew up Henry after he fell off his bicycle.

In August, 1940, we bought a new Chevrolet sedan. My mother and sister, Sarah Ramsey, came to Detroit. We saw the Tigers play two games and headed off on a whirlwind trip to Toronto, Ottawa, the Gaspe, Boston, and New York City. We had to see baseball games in each city after the sight seeing. The World's Fair was in New York, and of course we took it in for a day or two.

My Darling Margy

We arrived back in Tampa, where Frank and I continued our journey in Florida— to find a place to practice surgery. We visited Miami, Naples, Fort Myers, and Sarasota, and we both decided on Tampa. But in October 1940 an alternative offer came. It was an offer too good to turn down. Dr. Willard H. Parsons in Vicksburg, Mississippi, wanted a young, trained surgeon to join his hospital staff. This was a southern gentleman with Mayo Hospital training and a huge capacity for performing skilled surgery, writing papers, lecturing, traveling, and politics. Frank thought it would be a great opportunity, so after the interview he signed on for a year. It was a most productive year, and a year to meet many influential people in the medical world. It was a maturing year for both of us socially and professionally. Dr. Parsons kept telling me, "A wife can be a doctor's greatest asset." His wife, Edna Earle, a real southern charmer, was my mentor for many years.

At the end of the year, Dr. Parsons had treated Frank as a son and wanted him to stay with him. Frank still wanted a solo practice, so we said good-bye to Vicksburg. Frank already had a Florida license to practice, and we were going to start out in Tampa, my hometown, where we were welcomed with open arms.

We took an apartment, and found office space in the Citizen's Building on Franklin Street. With furniture and all new surgical equipment, we opened his office for the business of surgery in October. I was the only employee, taking the duties of secretary, technician, and nurse. We were soon busy, especially with night emergencies—Frank was getting all the accidents from the shipyards, and the older doctor friends called on him for their difficult cases. All this work and he wanted to get his surgical boards, and take exams to become a fellow of the American College of Surgeons. He applied and was told to take the exams in March, 1942.

But the Japanese attack on Pearl Harbor and Declaration of War in December of 1941 changed our lives. Frank volunteered for the US Army Medical Corps the next day. He was commissioned a captain and told to report for active duty in April, 1942. We closed the office, rented out the furniture and equipment, gave up our apartment, and Frank passed the exams in New Orleans. With our worldly possessions in our much traveled Chevrolet, we reported to duty at Camp Polk, Louisiana. The area was overrun with 500,000 troops on maneuvers. In two weeks we found a comfortable place to live after getting rid of the fleas—that was better than the bed bugs at the first place. At Camp Polk, where Frank was the only certified surgeon, he was assigned, instead, to the medical service. He served beyond the call of duty caring for the troops who had received contaminated yellow fever serum. Some soldiers were very sick, and a few died.

Frank heard of a new surgical unit being formed by the surgeon general, based on a new concept of having well-trained surgeons doing major surgery at the battle fronts where immediate treatment and surgery would save the severely wounded. Frank applied and was chosen to be in the Second Auxiliary Surgical Group. The group formed at Lawson General Hospital in Atlanta. For four months they hiked, rode horseback, pitched hospital tents, and became physically tough. They were a group of surgeons eager to see action. Frank was promoted to major and made commanding officer of a surgical team. He was off to the great adventure.

He left me in Atlanta bound for a secret embarkation point. Once in New Jersey, he sent off two quick letters before boarding. They're here before he starts keeping diary entries in a pocket-sized journal.

Feb. 24, 1943
8:30 P.M.
By Post
Sweetheart -

I don't know whether this note will reach you in time or not, but I'll try. The time has come and again we prepare. This time the trip will be quite different and exciting.

Please don't worry about me but think of me lots. I love you so much. I've always known it would be this way but even then it is so hard to leave you. I'll think and dream of you always, I love you with all my heart and soul.

Again, keep your chin up and wait for me. I'll come back to you someday -

I love you, dear

Frank

My Darling Margy

Feb. 25, 1943
By Post
My darling Margy-
      This is absolutely the last un-censored note I will be able to write you for some time to come. Mrs. Bowers will mail this in N.Y. for me.
      We are on the spot and long before you get this letter we will be on a big, fast boat going places.
      I'm sure I'll come back to you just as I left you, but at this time I want to tell you that you have been life itself for me. Whatever I did, whatever I was or may have been is all due to you. I have loved you dearly for over six beautiful years and I love you more now than I have even thought possible. If by any chance I don't see you again I have the thoughts and the memories of a most wonderful love and happiness with you. This is much harder on you than I, because you may have to go on living. I couldn't live without you.
      Please love me and think of me as I do you. I love you with all my heart and soul.
      When the going seems rough do as I do and will do. I will dream of you and have you with me in my soul. I know that will keep me going and be everything you want me to. I love you, I adore you and I want you — won't you do the same?
      We leave soon and will face a lot; I'll do every bit of my part because I'll feel that I'm doing it for us and what we love. I'm counting on you.
      I'll close and get this off. I'm writing this on the floor, as I don't have a bed, so please excuse.
      Love me as I love you
            Frank
      P.S. Tell Annie, R.L., Sara and Maynard Hello, and Goodbye.
                                          F.

～ ～

My Darling Margy

Diary of Major Frank Chunn 0-448722
Book Number One

February 26, 1943

Have been at our new camp for just a few days. Received orders to proceed. Time is short.

February 27

Left camp today and had a nice train trip with the unit. Train blacked out and we sang all during trip. Tonight we boarded an excellent large ship and after the march today we fell into bed. A good day and night.

February 28

We pulled out today and I guess we saw the last of the good ole U.S.A. today. Our ship is a large one and travels unescorted. However, we are well gunned and very fast. 5,000 men aboard and 66 nurses — what a scramble we will have !

March 1,

Ship is making excellent time. Straight course at night and zig-zag during day. Our first 20 hours run was 385 miles. There are many very sea sick people today. Have never felt better. Sighted a Destroyer at a distance. No Subs as yet. I am in charge of Life boat No. 11. It's a natural.

March 2,

Had an excellent night. Weather nice and balmy. Don't know where we are or where we are going but we are losing no time. This is a very fine English ship but it's dry as hell. We are still alone and I'd just as soon stay that way. Boat drill went well today and I now have 2 nurses to take in my boat. No subs as yet but excellent weather for them.

March 3,

A very interesting day, so far. Weather beautiful, ocean smooth and clear blue sky. Life boat drill as usual, afterward target parachutes were sent up and the anti-aircraft guns fired away. A most thrilling and excellent event to watch the rockets and tracer bullets, and also the heavy guns fire. We had many direct hits. Our gunners are good and God help the plane or sub we sight. Sea sickness on board is about gone and it's a real pleasure cruise.

March 4,

Another beautiful day. Much the same routine. Weather getting warmer and about all cases of sea-sickness are well. Ship's guns have been increased but the only thing we have seen so far are fish. Would be exciting to see a Sub !!!

March 5-

Weather continues to hold and the Ship's officers appeared in white this a.m. We are still in wools.

More gun fire today but only practice. No subs or planes. We know not where we are or where going. This a.m. at 5:30 a scream was heard from E deck. Some poor devil may have gone over-board. This ship stops for nothing. Well that's one way -. A good many still sleep in clothes but I enjoy my silk P.J.'s. Do you remember, Margy ?

Later: Last night we were chased by a Submarine but the Captain turned on full speed and we walked away from the little devil. Tomorrow will be quite a day —.

March 6 -

A great deal going on. This ship has been dodging all over the ocean. We were in a hot spot yesterday. The Subs were quite close and several in number. Due to this our course was greatly altered and we are a day behind in sailing time. However, we are still

My Darling Margy

intact and happy. The Skipper knows his stuff.

March 7 -
        Still dodging and doing a damn good job of it. Last night
was quite rough and the boat had quite a roll. Several more sea
sick people. Sighted three whales off Port side this afternoon. First
time I ever saw one and they gave us a good show — water works
and all. Our cruise is approaching its climax. Then the real fun
will begin. We are prepared for air attacks while landing. Issued
Army "C" rations today. A very nice dance aboard last evening
and I won at bridge. This has been a wonderful trip — I hate to
land —.

March 8 -
        Today is last full day aboard. Have had a wonderful crossing,
everything perfect. This a.m. we were greeted by two U.S. PBY-
3's flying boats. They have been over us all day and they give one
a safe feeling, however we haven't felt unsafe at all. Last night
we were up to full speed again and made some very acute turns
— almost roll you out of bed. This all because we encountered
a full lighted ship. They did not see us. We will land soon and
start a march. My first Atlantic crossing has been perfect in every
respect. I am now Chief of General Surgical Team No. 18.

March 9 -
        Landed today at Casablanca and was taken to the Majestic
Hotel by Army truck — no marching. The hotel is perfect. It is
in the middle of downtown Casablanca. On the sidewalk in front
of the Hotel is an excellent cafe and we sit there in the afternoons
and drink excellent red wine and watch a very colorful city pass in
review. I have never seen anything like this. One dollar is worth
50 francs and 50 francs will buy anything. Rapidly I'm learning
to speak French again and to sum up everything, this place is
perfect. Our rooms in the hotel are the best, and a funny thing,

every room is equipped with wash basin and a douche basin, of course in the bath room. These French know all the answers. Margy won't like this but we have a very pretty little French Chamber maid (Mode) who takes very good care of us. She draws the bath, washes my back but I do the drying. At 4:00 p.m. we dress and drink red wine at the sidewalk cafe. Then we get a Victoria carriage with the top down and ride through Casablanca, visiting with various people and on into the night. Nights here are so very beautiful. Moon, stars, music and wine. Margy, if you could only be here. It's like living in a dream. The French are very nice and the Arabs very dirty. For F50 we obtain an excellent bottle of wine, for F30 a carriage, and best of all, good ole American cigarettes for 50 cents a carton. At present we live as we like — sleep, eat and drink according to the mood. However, this won't last long. We go forward soon and some won't return. We are doing a lot of living now. There is so much to see, do and try to tell. I wish everyone could come here once. I'll write more tomorrow.

March 11,

Still having a swell time in Casablanca. Went through the Sultan's Palace today and he has some lay out.

Now I guess I can write it. On the 6th & 7th of March during the crossing, we were fired at twice with torpedoes from unseen Submarines. We did some plain and fancy dodging and ran 1400 miles off our course but the tin fish didn't get us. The event was exciting and gave us a change from the usual routine. The old boat was all right. I hope to go back on her unless we can fly. Bedding rolls arrived today.

2nd Aux. Surg. Gp. APO 3660 c/o Postmaster New York, NY
March 13, 1943
By Post
My darling,

We have been moved from the hotel and are now living in a tent camp. The honeymoon is over. Everything is rough and back to nature, but we still are having a fine time. Our food is excellent and occasionally we drink wine—there is no whiskey here. I think it's a good thing.

This city becomes more colorful every day. Last night I went out to an Arab café and had a wonderful meal—champagne, brook trout, and chicken cooked in wine. It took us about two hours for the meal. It was quite a time.

Black-out comes very early but we are able to get around as much and as late as we like. There are many shops here and many beautiful things. You would have a swell time looking around.

You should see me all dressed up in pinks and riding a bicycle down the Rue de Paris, and even better in a Victoria carriage in the afternoons. There is always something to do and a gang to go with. The other day I went through the Sultan's palace, and thought it very beautiful, especially the Harem!!!

Sweetheart, sometime we will come here on a second honeymoon and I'll show you so many interesting things. You will enjoy every minute of it. This so very different and seems to get better every day. We could have such good times here together. The nights are warm and beautiful. Of course, one has to watch his step, where he goes. The Medina is some place, but off limits.

The sleeping bag is just the thing now. I couldn't do without it. I don't need an air mattress. We get good American cigarettes for 5 cents a pack, wine for 4 cents a glass, meals for 70 cents a day. Beats Atlanta!! We also rent bicycles for $2 a week which is very high.

Oh, there is so much I want to tell you—and I will tell it all some day. It's like a beautiful color dream. I'll close for today. Be a good soldier and love me.

I love you so,
Frank
P.S. Give Annie and R.L. a big kiss from me.

2nd Aux. Surg. Gp. APO 3660 c/o Postmaster New York, NY
March 14, 1943
V Mail
Dearest Margy,

For once I've done a lot of letter writing. You will probably get them all at once. Our tent camp is going along nicely. Everything is in the open air, and shaving and bathing is with cold water. Guess I'll grow a full beard rather than pull them out as I have been doing.

Today is Sunday and we have just seen an Arab wedding and a funeral— both look about the same—a long line of Arabs and carriages and chanting all the way. This afternoon a group of us are going to the beach and play around in the sun. Doubt if we go swimming. Last night we went to the Officers Club on the [censored]. It's a nice place in an old French building. We heard American music and our waiter was a tremendous Negro from little ole Jacksonville, Fla. He gave us good service. I visited the 6th General Hospital yesterday to see Jim Mason. He has been sick since we left the States, but coming along fine now. Also visited the native hospital and saw some most unusual diseases. It's almost unbelievable. Our time in this place is about up, and I guess we will go [censored] soon. I understand it is even more interesting there.

Give my love to Annie, R.L., Sadie and Maynard. I love you so very much and wish I could be with you. It won't be too long. Write me all the news. We hear very little here.
I adore you,
Frank

March 18 -

We have been moved from our nice hotel and we are now in tents in camp. We are on the ground with nothing but cold water to bathe, shave in. The nights are quite cold and days warm. Our food is the best and plenty of it. Our big problem is bathing, shaving and clean clothes. We do our own laundry and have no pressing. I for one am having a big time and getting quite a kick

out of it. After dark the city is in complete black out. Curfew for
the natives is at 10 p.m. but we go around as long and late as we
like. It's something to be all dressed up and walking down the
Boulevard de la Gare on the Rue de Paris with a .45 Automatic
under your arm and a flashlight in your hand. So far we have
had very little trouble but nights are dangerous. Our life goes on
much the same. We have not started work as yet. We spend our
time on the beach, driving about the city and country, shopping
and having wine or champagne in the late afternoon at our
Sidewalk Cafe. All in all, it's fun.

March 19,

Last evening while having dinner at a native cafe (excellent
place) I ran into two Naval officers whom I had known at the
Tampa shipyard. Don't remember their names but we had a big
time. Today while walking down the Rue de la Gare I ran into
Nip Canipelli (Capt.,M.C.) from Ford Hospital. He is looking
fine and has been here some time. We plan to get together soon.

March 20,

Went through the Old Medina of Casablanca today and
I have never seen anything so dirty, so typical and so heart
breaking. Adults with every type of disease, children with eyes
out, extremities missing, malnourished and developed. They live
far worse than animals. We were conducted through five Brothels
or as we call them, whore houses. Strange to say these places were
cleaner and nicer looking than most of the homes. These places
are all under French government regulation and French soldiers
that have the desire are marched in formation to the Brothels and
sent in by their officers. The Army pays the fee — some system.
These places are "Off Limits" to American officers and soldiers.
Not so much from the angle of venereal disease but after dark in
the Medina is extremely dangerous for us. All in all an interesting
day. We are still living in Camp Lyeoty.

March 21,

This a.m. we were gotten up early and packed to move north to Rabat. Finally at 7:30 p.m. the trucks arrived and we made the trip in the rain to Rabat. On arrival we had hot coffee, spam and bread in the rain but it tasted very good. Our new camp is 3 1/2 miles from Rabat at an old race track site. It's a very pretty spot but, oh, so wet. Tomorrow I'll see what Rabat is like.

March 23 -

Rain continues and by now everything is either wet or damp. In our new camp we have tents and cots, no water or electricity. Each man is allowed one canteen and one helmet full of water a day for drinking, shaving and washing. We eat on the grass and live entirely in the open. Close by is a French Air field and there is much air activity about and after seeing the French planes one wonders how they even fly. Rabat is a very beautiful, colorful city — much more so than Casablanca. It's smaller than C , and quite clean. The city has an old wall around it which even today is in a fair condition. One enters the city through old gates in the wall. The French and the Arabs here are cleaner, dress better and appear of a much higher type than those in Casablanca. For the past two days I have been buying equipment for the camp from the stores of Rabat and have had many interesting events and met many nice people. My orders are quite large and I have U.S. money — therefore I get the best service and much native attention.

2nd Aux. Surg. Gp.APO 668 c/o Postmaster New York, NY
March 25, 1943
V Mail
My Darling Margy,
Since writing last we have moved north and are now living in the field in tents. We were quite busy getting moved and settled and it has rained for several days. Everything is wet, muddy, and cold.

                                    My Darling Margy

Again I say that sleeping bag is the best investment I ever made. So far we have received no mail. Hope you have heard from me. There is not much I can tell you except that the city we are close to is very nice and very clean—better than the one we left. However, life now is in the rough, living in tents with a dirt floor, candles for light, and three quarts of water a day for drinking, shaving, and washing. One learns to do on very little. I went in town the other day and had a wonderful eel and boar dinner with several things I never saw before.

Sweetheart, it's been so long since I've seen you and I miss you very much. Wish you were here to enjoy the country, but not the field life. I'll write again tomorrow. I love you, dearly,
Frank

～

March 27,

Our camp has been named Camp Tarfu — a very fitting name. If anyone wants to know why, I'll be very glad to explain. The food is the usual Army field rations and very good. I've learned how to take a complete bath in 1/2 helmet full of water and get clean. Last night Adkins and I had dinner at the Balima and had an excellent dinner complete with champagne. A few nights ago we tried to eat eel for dinner and thought it was foul. They then gave us boar which was about the best meat I have ever eaten. It looks like the Nurses will be moving out in camp with us soon. So far they have been quartered in a hotel down town. We'll see how the females can take it.

March 29 -

Today our nurses moved into camp and will for their first time start roughing it. This should be very funny.

March 30.

Tomorrow is pay day and everyone is patiently waiting 'til tomorrow night. Should be a good party at the Balima. Had a

busy day doing a lot of trading with several French and Arab
merchants. I speak little to no French and they speak no English
but we trade up a storm and so far I've come out O.K. I have been
buying equipment for camp.

The H.M.T. *Andes* came in today from New York and
brought mail but I was not in luck. Perhaps next time. It's a
lonesome feeling and it's been over a month with no word from
home. Adkins and Swingle got letters. Had a good horseback ride
yesterday and several good games of badminton today. Yesterday
was one of tension here in Rabat. The Free French and the Vichy
French had a big meeting and some trouble. We were warned and
so packed a .45. Had no difficulty. The past few days have been
fine. Hot during the day and cold at night. They say this is a cold
country with a hot sun — I believe it.

I miss you more than ever tonight Margy — I love you so.

March 31 -

A red letter day for me. Today I received my first letters from
home. Two letters from Margy and letters never looked so good
to me before. Even a bill from home would look good now. From
what Margy writes, the first 14 letters from her have been lost.
Hope mine are getting through.

The French airfield next door is a busy place today. The Frogs
are doing a lot of flying. There was a good bit of gun fire last
night over toward the beach. Don't know as yet what it was, but
gun fire doesn't bother us anymore — not unless it's too close.
Today is pay day.

April 5 -

Nothing unusual has happened in past few days. We hear we
are to move up to the front soon and help clean up Rommel. That
should be a good show with lots of work to do. We shall see !

Last night Capt. Swingle and I were in Rabat at the Tout Va
Bien for dinner and had a very fine time, however coming back

                                          My Darling Margy

to camp in the black-out and without a flashlight, I fell flat into
a bomb shelter trench. Didn't get hurt but my only clean clothes
got dirty as hell. This morning the boys are having a big time
kidding me. The story is very colored by now. Anyhow the dinner
and champagne was fine. Water rations were cut a couple of days
back but we are doing O.K.

April 7, 1943

Had a nice trip to Casablanca yesterday. Took two patients
down in an ambulance to the 6th General Hospital from the 51st
Station Hospital. Had all afternoon to do as I wanted in C. with
a driver and transportation. Saw several old friends and ran into
Dan Ellis, a class mate from Duke. By the best of luck I sort of
wandered into the French Wine Ration Office and met a very
nice French lady who after a cigarette gave me an order of 10
bottles of champagne at 16 francs a bottle ($.32). I am invited
back for more. Later I drove out to the 8th Evac. Hospital and
saw several friends I knew at Camp Kilmer. Later I came back
by the 6th General and picked up Jim Mason, who was just
discharged from hospital and brought him back to camp. Last
night we sampled the bubble water and it's fine. No mail today.

April 9, 1943

Today the sunrise was the most beautiful and most welcome
of my life so far. I say this in re' of what I'm about to write. It
could be made into an interesting book but I'm not a writer so
I'll just note the high spots. I still think I'm lucky to be alive.
Yesterday afternoon I dropped in at the Balima (Rabat) for a
drink. After having two or three Muscat I went to the men's
room and while in there met a very handsome young Arab. He
seemed to be a very high type Arab — very well dressed in his
native clothing and very nice. I invited him to have a drink at
my table. While drinking we were joined by Capt. Moore (2nd
Aux.) and a bit later by a second Arab who was a friend of Abbis,

the fellow I had just met. Abbis' friend's name was Hassan.
Capt. Moore, Abbis, Hassan and I had several drinks and talked,
mostly in French. At 6 p.m. I invited all to have dinner with me.
Our dinner was excellent and when the last wine glass was empty
it was 10 p.m. Abbis then invited Capt. Moore and me to come
to his home in the Old Medina. (The Old Medina of Rabat is
"Off Limits" to Americans and very dangerous to Americans
— especially after dark. Extremely few American officers have
ever been in the Medina at night.) Moore and I talked it over and
decided to take a chance and go. So with our two Arab friends
whom we had just met we strolled down to the Medina gates
and got by the M.P.'s by wearing the Arabs' Fez and ducking
our caps and walking in the middle. After getting through the
gate we were led through many dark, narrow, winding and dirty
streets and walks. Arabs were all through the place, standing in
the doorways and in the shadows. Anyway, Abbis and Hassan
got us safely to Abbis' home. We found ourselves in one of the
most beautiful Arab palaces I have ever seen. The rooms were
very large with ceilings two and three floors high. The floors were
tile and the walls were inlaid marble. Beautiful rugs on the floor
and we sat on very low, soft couches or large pillows on the floor.
We met Abbis' father, brothers, cousins, etc. but saw none of the
women of the house. Abbis' father was the Morac Judge of the
Sultan. We sat, talked and smoked with him. Then a 12 piece
native orchestra was playing in the next room. We went in and
listened and were served hot, Arab tea (excellent) and cookies,
fruits, and cakes. (We were allowed to keep our shoes on.) Then
we were taken upstairs to a beautiful room where we ate and
drank more and all in all, had a wonderful time. We were then
invited to spend the night as the hour was late. I knew damn well
we should not but I wanted to see what it was like. After all I had
heard of no American ever spending the night in the Medina.
I accepted the invitation and so did Moore. It seemed to make
them happy. Anyway we were taken to a large, beautiful bedroom

                                        My Darling Margy

with six beds. Three beds at each end and the beds were built like
steps. A high bed, a medium and a low bed all pushed together.
There were many large, soft beautiful pillows and colored silk
hand worked sheets and beautiful native wool blankets. As I
was the ranking officer I was given the high bed to sleep on and
Moore the medium bed. We were brought beautiful Arab night
gowns, all hand worked. Moore and I went to bed wondering just
what in the hell we had gotten ourselves into. Had a fine sleep
and woke at 7:00 a.m. still alive. We thanked our host and told
them we were in a rush to get back to camp and so didn't stay for
breakfast. Abbis and Hassan took us to the gates of the Medina
and as good luck would have it, there were no M.P.'s in sight.
We came back to camp. I'm certainly glad I went last night and
promise myself I won't go again. I saw and did things last night
that I had only heard and read about before. They really exist and
it was just like an Arabian Nights dream. The gang at camp was
astounded when Moore and I told them our story.

April 10 -
    Well, here goes again ! Last afternoon at the Balima, Moore
and I met Abbis and Hassan again. They invited us to their
home for dinner. We told them that it was impossible for us to
get a pass to go into the Medina. Hassan then sent to his home
in the Medina and had the dinner transported to his summer
villa outside of the Medina. Moore and I were taken by carriage
to Hassan's villa and had a wonderful Arab dinner. We sat on
pillows on the floor, crossed our legs and ate off of a table one
foot high. No silver was on the table and we ate with our right
hand only. The food was good and of course in Arab style. I'm
not sure what we ate but we had fun. Everyone ate out of the
same large plate with their hands. Many courses were served and
different kinds of wine were put before us. Some of the dishes
were chicken, pork, lamb, whole grain wheat, and some sort of
beans. The bread was black and coarse but good. After the meal

a servant brought a basin with soap, water and towel to wash our hands with. It was an unusual experience and I'm glad I went but G.I. food is better. I'm invited to an Arab dance next week. Hope I can make it.

April 13 -

Today my surgical team was put on the alert and told that we would probably be going to the front. Several other teams were also included and we are feeling very good over the prospects. Adkins, Swingle and I will evidently still be together. I checked my surgical instruments and find most everything I will need. Camp goes on as usual and we see quite a bit of Rabat.

April 15 -

Still on the alert and nothing else has happened. I went to Casablanca today and had a very fine time. Saw several friends and was invited to a party for Sunday next. Sorry I won't be able to get there. I brought back another case of champagne. It's very good and through the French government is very cheap. No major events lately, just the usual camp life and race-tracking.

~ ~

2nd Aux Surg Gp, APO 521 NY NY
April 17, 1943
V Mail

My darling-
I'm still trying to write on my lap and its not so good. In the past two or three days I have received most of your letters. However, there are several still missing- perhaps they will yet arrive. Thanks for sending some of the new calling cards. They are very nice. As to what to do about Dodo [a car] — Sweet, do just as you think best. Anything will be OK with me. In many of your letters you ask me to cable you. I have tried this as many of us have and so far its impossible. No

                                    My Darling Margy

matter what the reason I certainly hope that by now that you have heard from me and know I am safe and happy. Why in the hell our safe arrival cards were not sent out, I don't know. When I get home I'll find out why. Keep using the APO numbers as I send them to you. We have changed often and perhaps more. Darling I love you and miss you with all of me
Frank

❧ ❧

April 19 -

Nothing much new. Col. Forsee returned from the front last night and we expect (my team) to go out soon. I have been on the alert for several days. In re' of our departure, Adkins and I drank the last two bottles of champagne and had quite a time. I finally had to put him to bed. Two days from now we will start taking quinine routinely.

April 21 -

Today my team was put on the alert and we expect flying orders anytime. I'm going to the front with an English outfit. I guess I won't write just where or when at this time but will later. We will take about a 900 mile trip by plane and then really go to work. It sounds great and I'm sure we will have quite a time. It's just like the night before Christmas. Today, I took several more vaccinations and last night began taking Atabrine and will continue. We have no quinine. This looks like the beginning of the end for the Axis in Africa and I'm going to be in on the kill. Then what, I wish I could write my thoughts. Margy, if I don't come out of this little trip, please understand that I wouldn't change it if I could and that I love and adore you. So long for now.

❧ ❧

APO 521, NY NY
April 25, 1943
V Mail

My darling wife-
Today is Easter Sunday and I've missed you more than ever today. The Easter Parade is about the same here as home only not as nice. Everyone in town was out in their best if not new clothes. I miss so not being able to be with you. You will never know how it is. The bad part also was that last night I either lost my bill-fold or it was stolen. Every franc I had was in it along with your picture and my identification card. I'm broke and blue but thank goodness it's only a week til payday. Your new allowance will come through on May 1st 1943. Please let me know about it. I could use some now, ha ha.

As I told you in my last letter don't be worried if you don't hear from me for a little while. You keep writing to the above APO. Yes, we have lots of rabbit here [clue that he was in Rabat] but not for long. Please remember on your trip east to say hello to Ben as you pass through. I would like to see him.

My darling, I love you so very much and miss you with all my heart. Be sweet,
Frank
RL and Annie- hey!

❦

April 25, 1943 Easter Sunday

We remain at Rabat but are red hot. We expect to fly to Bone, Algeria, in one or two days to start work in the 5th General English Hospital. Seems like the big push is beginning and we will be in it. Can hardly wait. But, oh hell, something bad did happen last night or during the night. I lost my billfold with Margy's picture, my identification card and pay data card and last but not least over 6000 francs ($120). I'm one broke bird and just about to take a long trip. That's the worst thing about the war so far except of course being away from home. Guess it will all come out in the wash.

11:00 p.m.

Orders just came in and I'm to take my team to the front (Bone, Algeria). The big push on Tunis has started and we are to take part in it. I have to pack everything, get instruments and leave Rabat at 4:00 a.m. tomorrow for Casablanca. There my team and 5 other teams will fly to Algeria, then on to Bone to the 5th General Hospital British for duty. Two teams will stop at Algiers, two at Phillipeville and two at Bone. Bone is at the front. Must pack now.

April 26, 1943 — April 27, 1943

Had a wonderful trip by plane today. We went by truck from Rabat to Casablanca and there we left in 3 planes for Algiers, Algeria. We stopped at Oran for dinner and then flew on to Algiers where we spent the night in the 29th Station Hospital. Next morning 4 teams boarded 2 planes and flew east to Bone, Algeria. Two teams were left in Algiers.

On arriving in Bone no one was expecting us and I hitch-hiked a ride for my two teams to the 5th General Hospital British and sent the remaining two surgical teams on to the 67th General Hospital British in Phillipeville, Algeria, by truck. We (my 2 teams) arrived at the 5th General Hospital in time for afternoon tea. The hospital is a 1000 bed tent hospital 18 miles southeast of Bone. Its name is a general hospital but really it's an evacuation hospital and is well forward. We are blacked-out at night and look for air raids. At 9:30 p.m. we had an air raid during which 3 German planes were shot down. We stood in front of our tent and watched the entire show. The sky was filled with search lights, bursting shells and tracer bullets. Must have lasted 15 to 20 minutes. Bombs were dropped but fell in the sea and did us no harm. It was quite a show and well worth seeing. I understand they are quite frequent here.

April 28

Busy today getting set up and ready to go to work. Went in to Bone on business and the town is a shattered wreck. Everything that is still standing is closed and boarded up. Very few people on the streets except soldiers. No shops are open. Seems like a nightmare. Expect to go to work in 1 or 2 days.

April 29 -

Our operating theater is now ready for action and we are waiting on patients to be brought in. I went in to Bone today and managed one way or the other to obtain some medical supplies and U.S. Army food (cans). Our food is so much better than the British. Here they serve us tea 4 times a day and no coffee. Just heard the air raid alarm. Wonder what kind of show this is going to be. Somehow the British don't seem to mind air raids and since being here with them I believe I understand why air raids would never lick England. They are a fine bunch even though I don't agree with a lot of their surgery. Have seen a good many German prisoners pass through here and many are patients. I must say they are good patients. Even met and talked to one from Philadelphia who seems to be pro-American.

Today, I received a message from the 95th General Hospital British that my wallet had been found intact and was being sent to me. The 95th is in Algiers and I lost my wallet in Rabat. Can't understand how it happened but I'm glad it did.

Strange things happen over here.

May 1, 1943

Today is May Day and I have been in the Army one year today. A year usually is quite a little time, but this one has been so short and so very full.

Today I look like a British officer. I'm wearing the British Army shorts, shirt and knee stockings with gaiters. My nurses had a fine laugh when I walked into the operating theater this a.m.

My Darling Margy

However, the clothes are cool and very comfortable. The only difference between me and the British is the insignia. I'm already talking like them — can't seem to help it.

Talked to Col. Stark (Bn.C.O.) today and I'm going to take a trip up to the front lines and see what to hell it's all about. I'll go up to the lines at Tunis. I'll take a Tommy Gun along — I understand it's open season !!!

Margy, I'm glad you don't know this 'cause you would certainly raise the devil, but I must see it.

Another air raid was headed our way last night but was evidently headed off — dammit.

❧ ～ ❧

2nd Aux. Surg Gp. APO 521 c/o Postmaster New York NY
May 1, 1943
By Post
My Darling Wife,
It's just before dinner and I thought I would write you another letter. I was lying on the cot trying to get a nap but kept thinking of you and wanting to see you. Then I got out the map, and Gee, I'm a long way from home and you. I've been away from you for about two and a half months now, and it seems like years. God only knows how much longer it will be before I see you again. I'm in hopes that it won't be so long as we expected. Anyway, we will be good soldiers and carry on til that time comes. It will be wonderful coming back to you. I want you to meet me at the boat and we'll have a grand time, just you and I, for as long as we like. Then we will go on back by Asheville and then to Tampa and start all over again. After this, I will have learned many things about life and living and I know that you are the most important thing in it. Sounds like I'm homesick, does it not? I miss you and all, but I couldn't have missed this.

Darling, I'm sure you understand, and I believe you feel the same way and wanted to come along. By all means, don't join the "WACs", etc., and go on foreign duty. It's no place for a girl to be, and I don't want you to do it. I want you as you were when I come back home.

I'll do our part.

We are having quite a storm just now, and it's so dark I'm writing with a flash light, and it's only 5:45 pm. Guess we won't have any air raids tonight due to the heavy storm. Guess that will be OK, too.

The other day in the plane I saw a couple of periscopes following a ship. Didn't have time to see anything else and didn't know whose they were. Anyway, the sea here is very beautiful. We must make this sea cruise some day, and I don't mean ocean. [clue – the Mediterranean Sea]

The rain continues and this camp will be a muddy mess before long.

* * *

I went on to dinner and just got back covered with mud. I'm wearing my new shorts, however, and saved my pants. From now on we'll have to do our own washing, and pressing is out. I won't look so dressed up until we get back to civilization.

The British serve four meals a day, including tea at 4:30 pm. It really amounts to a meal. They do very well with what they get, but they don't get the food we do. They have no coffee at all, only tea. Two or three days ago I went down to one of our food dumps and got a case of coffee, milk, peaches, and a case of pineapple. The British officers and we enjoyed it very much, and I made quite a hit with them.

In one of your letters you asked what a medina was. The medina is the native Arab part of a city, enclosed by a high ancient wall. Medina and casbah are the same. Remember the radio play? Well, anyway, I have a great story to tell you about the medina. It would be a chapter in anybody's life.

This letter seems to go on and on, but for some reason I just want to write to you. Haven't heard from you in over a week now, but I expected that. Your letters will have to be forwarded to me after they reach 521 and that will be slow. Hope mine continue to reach you without much delay.

                                    My Darling Margy

In the other places I was learning to speak French, but since the move I am only with the British, and so am learning English with accent and expressions. They are excellent people and I enjoy being with them.

So put two and two together and think of Rudy, ha ha. [The dog's name was a clue that he was near Bone, Algeria.]

Sweetheart, I have to go operate a bit, and then I think I will go to bed and dream of you. I wish so that I could be with you tonight. We could have so much fun, and I could hold you close all through the night until dawn. I would be so happy if only for just one day or night.

Goodbye for now, Darling, and give Annie and R.L. my love and ask them to write sometime. Let me know when your increased allotment came through. Bye, Sweet, I love you with all of me.
Your
Frank

May 2, 1943

Today I was quite lucky and was able to obtain an Army 3/4 ton truck and a driver for personal transportation. Still don't know how I got it 'cause many a Col. around here is on foot. Anyway, I'll be able to get around a bit and see the country. There are many places I want to go and one place is the front lines. We are just back of them and I think I'll go on up soon. It's nice being your own boss again. I visited the 76th General Hospital British today and had a very fine time. Their C.O. is very interested in America and we had a nice talk. I believe I left him with the impression that the best thing about America is Florida. I'm invited back for dinner this week.

Last night we were invited to the Sgt's. Mess after dinner and I want to say it's the best thing in the British Army. We had excellent Scotch whiskey and music and singing. The Sgt's. Mess is quite a tradition and what a time we did have. I'm afraid I got nice and tight. As we say, I hung one on and the Col. was about one step ahead of me. We hit it off fine together but he is going to be sent back to England soon.

May 4th

Today I met a Lt. Mathers from Lake City and Tampa, Fla. Margy, he went to Plant High School but didn't know you. He did know R.L. and lots of other people I know. Had a fine chat. I'm going out to his outfit for dinner soon.

Today we admitted 500 new wounded from the Front, some with such severe wounds. One poor British soldier has a portion of his skull and brain blown away and is still able to talk very well, but is paralyzed on left side. It seems that the worst wounds are inflicted by the trench mortar. Tonight is an excellent night for an air-raid. Perhaps we'll be busy all night. The 76th General Hospital British will pull out in the a.m. to go on forward. Tonight I had a new dish, English curry, and it's quite good.

May 7th

It's rained like hell here for several days and I've lived in mud. Today I operated and treated patients all day long standing in mud up to my shoe tops. My hospital ward tents are like swamps. The wounded are really pouring in and it's one hell of a sight. Young fellows, American, British and German, shot to pieces with terrible wounds. Part live and some die — for what ?

Yesterday, I met Popsy's Private Army. It's the most fabulous outfit I've ever heard of. A Russian stock broker living in Egypt has financed a private Army of his own. He is called Popsy. His army consisted of 40 men at the beginning and at present is 17 strong. They travel in G.I. jeeps, either one or two and live six months out of the year behind the enemy lines blowing up bridges, exploding Ammo. dumps, cutting German throats and in general just raising hell with the enemy. How they get through the lines no one knows but they come and go at will. They

My Darling Margy

wear all sorts of uniforms and fight with everything. They have adopted the American 77th Evac. Hosp. as their resting place when on this side of the lines. That is where I met them.

This outfit of 17 men plus equipment traveled 500 miles across Tripoli in one small jeep in advance of the British 8th Army. They did this by riding and walking in relays, a sort of a shuttle system with the jeep, and I must say a bunch of real fighters.

It's cold and wet. Goodnight.

May 8th

In a big hurry, am going into Tunis for the kill. Hope I get back but if I don't, Margy, I love you with all my heart but can't resist this. — So long — perhaps.

May 11, 1943

Sweetheart, I'm back and am intact. My trip was one I'll never forget. Since my last note I've traveled 450 miles in my truck, was sniped at in Bizerte and shelled on Tunis road; then when I got back to our hospital we were shot up there. Had three patients killed and seven others wounded.

Now to start with, on May 8th I took the truck that I obtained (sort of a left handed borrow) got Walt Byers, McEwing and Col. Powers (British) and with a Tommy Gun and M-1 rifle and a .45 we started for the front. Officially to study the methods of evacuation of patients but actually to see what to hell it was like. Our first day we went up the Algerian and Tunisian coast road from Bone to LaCalle to Tebarka and on to Mateur. Mateur had just been taken by the Americans and there was fighting on up the Ferryville road so we stayed the night just west of Mateur at the 15th Evac. Hospital. While here I met and talked with General Kirk, the new Surgeon General. That night we almost froze but were up at dawn and drove on to Ferryville which had just fallen. The people in the streets threw roses and

all sorts of flowers in our truck and were dressed in their best
clothes and having a wonderful time because the Americans had
come. Then we rushed on to Bizerte. We entered Bizerte with the
Infantry — had our tin hats well on and Tommy Gun in hand.
Sniping was going on all over the city but no shelling. We went
on into the heart of Bizerte and had a look around. It is the most
bombed, shelled and wrecked city I've ever seen. Col. Power said
it was much worse than the cities in England. There was no one
there except the American soldiers mopping up. I went in several
wrecked buildings and found a nice present for Margy. After
a while we left the city proper. Due to the sniping went by the
harbor and saw several large ships burning and then went into
the German air drome. Our fliers certainly did a complete job in
wrecking it. Numbers of German planes were wrecked and the
large hangars were bombed to the ground. Here we picked up a
German machine gun and a beautiful operating room light. We
then drove on back to Ferryville and were at the Headquarters of
the I Armored Division when three German Generals came in
and gave up. It was quite a moment. We had dinner in the field
with an American clearing station unit and then started for Tunis.
We got 15 miles down the Ferryville-Tunis road and found that
some German units had not quit fighting and when we reached
the cross roads we found ourselves under shell fire. That is an
experience all its own. We got the hell out quick but not before
I got a Jerry helmet. When we were out of shell fire we stopped
and watched a tank battle over on the side of the hill. Then
the biggest surprise of all came. Thousands of Germans began
coming down the road in their trucks, ambulances and anything
that would roll, many walking. They had their equipment but
no arms. They were surrendering and damn glad to do so. Many
came up to us and wanted to surrender to us. We just waved them
on toward Ferryville. Some 30,000 must have passed us and the
road was jammed with German prisoners, American troops and
natives. We drove through the battle field and saw many German

                                   My Darling Margy

dead, lying where they had fallen, some blown to pieces. Animals were dead and dying, tanks knocked out and burning. There were German guns, helmets and equipment scattered all over the field. It was truly hell but our boys gave them a dose of their own medicine and in no uncertain terms. It was a real Yankee Victory and I was lucky enough to have seen it and come back. We captured a great quantity of equipment.

Again we tried to get to Tunis but heavy shelling along the road prevented our passing and so we joined the ever increasing stream of German prisoners and came back to Ferryville then to Mateur. From Mateur we drove to Beja and on the western side of Beja we stopped for supper at the 38th Evac. Hosp. and had supper with Paul Sanger, Dick Query, Stokes and Colon Monroe, Milo Hoffman and some others I've forgotten. On our way to Beja we came down "long stop hill" officially Hill 609 when a day or so before we had a tough and costly battle with the Jerries.

The Americans had to advance up a long, rolling mountain against German tanks and hidden field guns. It cost in American blood but they took it and the battle of "Long Stop Hill" will live in American tradition. This battle field also was bloody hell. Soldiers were digging graves and burying the dead. Little white crosses were on every hillside and many fine American lads are six feet under on these Tunisian hills. The whole of Africa is not worth the graves I saw that day. Anyway, enough of that. To continue we drove on to Sauk-el-Khomis and then to Sauk-el-Arba and then to Babouch, La Calle and back to our hospital east of Bone. We were tired, dirty and even sick at heart from some of the things we had seen. Byers vomited when he got out of the truck. We had come back safely and were just relaxing when we had an air raid. During the raid three A.A. shells fell about the hospital and killed two of my patients and wounded seven others. One of my wards was riddled and torn with shell fragments. One of my patients who I had put a leg cast on for a minor ankle fracture had the top of his head blown off. Miss Bennet, my nurse, had a very near miss. A shell fragment hit the ground a foot from where she was lying. (We all were flat on the ground when we heard the shells coming.)

Then we started work in the operating room and worked till dawn patching wounded up. I'm dead tired now but had to make these notes first. Goodnight.

May 12- Today I got many German and British wounded and have operated all day. I removed many bullets and shell and bomb fragments and tonight while operating the lights went off. I operated while my nurse held a flash light over the incision. Not the best conditions under which to operate !! The African campaign is now concluded and we are glad it's over and I'm happy that I could do my bit. What and where next ?

Diary of Major Frank Chunn
Book Number Two

May 13, 1943

We were bombed again last night with minor damage. Today while I was in Bone we had a raid. We were caught in the middle of it so I just found a nice corner and had a close up view of the raid. Shells began bursting directly overhead and the fragments raining down. At this stage of the game we pulled out and drove up on a little hill where the A.A. batteries were. They make a hell-of-a noise. We returned safely.

May 14th Another air raid tonight, but it was on a rather small scale and no bombs hit the city but did hit an American Liberty ship in the harbor. The fire was controlled and the ship saved. Several sailors, however, were killed.

May 15th. I have just finished 12 hours straight of operating. I started last night at 10 P.M. and finished this morning at 10 A.M. We had a nasty air raid last night and one Jerry plane with its full bomb load was shot down and landed in an American bivouac area. We had 48 admissions from the explosion and God only knows how many were killed outright. I amputated two legs, repaired many compound arm fractures and leg fractures. Many fragments were removed from various regions of others. It was a bloody job and an awful sight to see. My enlisted men got sick in turns. They are so jumpy now that they hardly sleep at night. My nurses are taking it fine. The other team relieved me this a.m. and in a few hours I'll go back and start again. There are some still to do and we have had more admissions today.

May 15 5:00 p.m.

Had another air raid about 2 hours ago. Seems like they come morning, noon and night now. Two shells came crying over our tents but thank God they didn't explode. I've learned to hit the ground in nothing flat when shells come our way. I just found out that we shot down three Jerries in last night's raid. Guess poor old Bone is in for a hell-of-a plastering in the next days to come. This afternoon I treated 8 Americans who were badly burned. I believe I'll have to amputate another leg tonight.

10:00p.m. May 15th.

Another God damn air raid. It's getting so one can't get a damn bit of rest. It's all night ducking in a dirty fox hole. I don't give a bloody damn about the bombs but I haven't had any sleep in about 2 days. The only consolation we have is that this a.m. 400 of our planes passed over going to bomb hell out of Italy. Probably will operate all night again.

May 17 — I've been very busy for the past two days. We were raided again last night and the night before. Yesterday and today I operated all day long and have many cases to do tomorrow. It seems there is no end to this business. Some of our teams are being called back to Rabat. Perhaps the next big show is to be soon.

May 19th 8:00p.m. I've just finished 35 hours of operating and am a bit tired. Today I operated on 33 cases, not counting yesterday and last night. I have two little ole American nurses who stuck right with me all the long hours and worked like hell. I've never heard one complaint and when we finished tonight they could still smile. They are grand girls and real soldiers. I'll never be able to say enough for the American Nurse. They shouldn't be here. It's no place for them but they are here and are doing their part. Some bastards in the States that I know should see them. Well, enough of that. Tonight is a beautiful moon light night and

                                    My Darling Margy

I guess we won't have any air raid and can spend several hours sleeping. Don't think I would move tonight if a bomb came into the tent. I would give any price for a cold "Coke" just now or an orange. Goodnight.

May 21st. Last night we were having a little party in my tent with several of the British officers and our nurses. We were having a fine time drinking scotch and talking when all of a sudden all hell broke loose over us. As one man we all hit the ground and several drinks of Scotch were lost. This one didn't last very long so we continued the party and a big time was had by all. However, this a.m. the C.O. said we made too much noise, etc. I have two German and two Italian Medical Officers now. They, of course, are prisoners and are doing ward duty on my German and Italian wards. Our Italian is a Lt.Col. and a very nice fellow. They carry out my orders very well and we get along fine. Strange things happen. We have about caught up on the rush and perhaps can take it a bit easy for a while. All depends on the air raids. I heard last night from Algiers that the 2nd Aux. had moved to Oran. Perhaps we are getting ready for the push across the Pond. I understand we are going. The sooner we do the sooner we get home.

May 25- Had a hell of a night last night. Several of us started out in a 2 1/2 ton truck to drink beer on the beach (Mediterranean). Got about 8 miles from camp and got stuck in the mud. We took off our pants and waded out. We were in mud to our hips, to put it politely, and walked back to camp. This a.m. I took a British truck driver down to pull mine out and by damned if it didn't get stuck. After much labor and mud we got both out. This afternoon I had a sedan and put on pinks and blouse and had a wonderful drive around Bone and the countryside. Went to the old French Garrison, to the French Hospital, and through the Casbah. We ended up at my little special cafe for a bottle of Vin Rosie.

Last night was bad but today was excellent. I just counted up my records and last week I did 170 operations and about as many the week before. They were performed on Americans, British, Germans, Italians and Arabs. It's some mixture but the treatment works on all.

One of our big problems is maggots in wounds. They look like hell and worry the patients but they do clean up a wound. We don't, by the way, put the maggots there. When we dress a maggots wound usually everyone in the operating theater gets sick. Goodnight.

May 24th Had another air raid tonight. It was quite a long one and I was operating at the time. Had a time keeping my enlisted men off the floor when the shells were bursting overhead. I guess after being shot up as we have no one can blame a man for wanting to get down. I've come to believe that only one may have your name on it and then ducking won't do much good so I go wearily along and say what-to-hell.

It's getting hot as blue blazes now. It was around 105 degrees in my tent today, sort of takes the pep out of one. I hate to think what it will be in August.

May 25- Had two air-raids last night and saw one plane come down in flames- not a pretty sight. I was operating during the first raid and had to do most of a tough appendectomy by flashlight when the lights went out. It was funny at that. When things got a bit near, I had a job keeping my enlisted men off the floor. Of course, the floor was the place to be but I had to have help for the operation. Everything came out all right including the appendix. During the second raid I was too sleepy to get out of bed so turned over and went to sleep. It would be nice if I had a deaf ear, I could put the good one on the pillow and sleep on through. Sure would like to have a Coca-Cola.

May 29 — The work goes on as usual and so do the bombings.
Last night we had quite a raid with the usual number of shells
hitting around us. Jerry dropped magnesium flares over us
and evidently took pictures. He will probably come back again
tonight. We saw Beau-fighters attack the enemy planes last night
and drive them across the Mediterranean. One of my men has a
sprained ankle from jumping in a fox hole during last nights raid.
So far no more shells have hit us. Today I horse traded the Padre
(British Chaplain) out of a quart of Scotch and 3 bottles of beer
for some soap. Some system ?

Yesterday my bed roll arrived and I now have some clean
clothes, the first in about 6 weeks. I think I'll dress up, go to the
Village and eat Kush-Kush.

May 31st Things have hit an all time low. I can't write it home so
I'll just write it in the diary and perhaps I'll feel better. For the
past 3 days I've had a severe finger infection. Day before yesterday
I took gas and the finger (left thumb) was incised and drained.
Since then it has hurt like hell and I'm loaded to the gills on
sulfadiazine. The weather is so damn hot and with all this at once
I've felt completely washed out. The work has to go on and I can't
quit now. This morning Mac Ewing, my assistant, came down
with a fever and very sore throat. This heat is hell on him with his
fever. Also the food status is getting bad. The British just don't
have it and we go hungry a great deal of the time. We have so
many German and Italian prisoners to feed. Vitamins are a thing
of the past. This probably explains the increase in our infections
and illnesses.

For the moment our team is about shot but I'm sure will
recover completely in a few days. I'd give a month's pay for a fresh
5 or 10 pound beef steak and fried potatoes.

Now I feel better and won't gripe again. It must be the effect
of the sulfadiazine cause I'm glad I'm here and until the war is won
for us I wouldn't go home for anything. Of course I want to but
my job now is here.

June 2, 1943 The thumb is still sore and painful, but am able to be about. Yesterday I did 10 cases (operative) with one hand. I had the nurse be my left hand and managed. Ewing is still in bed with a fever, probably malaria. Capt. Jarvis is very ill today with diarrhea and vomiting. My enlisted man (tech) has been very sick for 2 days with severe diarrhea. For the moment the group is laid up, but hope they are all well soon. I continue on aspirin, sulfadiazine and scotch in order to sleep at all. This damn thing has really hurt.

Boys and girls, the indications are that the really big show is about to begin. I think we will be taking a little boat trip across the Mediterranean soon. That should be a hot stretch of water with plenty to do and see.

⌁

2nd Aux. Surg. Gp.APO 521 New York, NY
June 4, 1943
By Post
My Darling,
Again my birthday has come and gone, and I was given a nice party by the British Sisters (nurses), American nurses, and British officers. We went down to MY little French café and had a good meal and Scotch and soda. When the café owners found out it was my birthday, they came over and kissed me on both cheeks. There were five of them including the cook—I was well kissed. We then ate a very good French dinner with vin rose. After dinner we all sat around and sang American and British songs. The English and French seem to enjoy our parties a great deal.

I have become quite good friends with this family (French) that run the café, and enjoy their food so much. They are always inviting me to eat with them and call me "mon petit commandant." When things are quiet we have such fine times there. The mayor of the town usually drops in to have a drink with us, and I guess we could have the town if we wanted it. He is very fond of the Americans.

Our group has gotten along very well here and we have

My Darling Margy

become well known. Our work is light now, and we have more time to do various things and get around a bit. Swimming in the Mediterranean is wonderful, and drives through the mountains are very nice.

Many of my German patients ask me if they are going to be sent to America—they all want to go to America. They are disappointed when I tell them I don't know where they will go. I have several Polish soldiers who were forced into the German army and captured here. They hate the Germans, and are glad they are in our hands.

In other letters, I told you about seeing the big event here. I was at the front in those days, and saw many interesting things happen. I was at a well known city the day the Germans surrendered and came into our lines. Many tried to give themselves up to our group, but we just moved them on back. I've never seen such a sight. However, the worst thing of all was the fresh battle field as we went in. It's not a pretty picture.

We went into a German hospital just after it was captured. They had not had time to evacuate the patients, and we saw everything intact, including the medical officers.

This visit was very interesting even though we got in several hot spots. I have a great tale to tell you sometime, Sweetheart, but the most important thing is for you not to worry about me. I can take care of myself and certainly will. I am in good health, quite tan and dirty, but happy and having a fine time.

I understand that the ship I came over on was sunk—and I thought she was too fast for that. Several weeks ago I had dinner on an American ship (I told you about it) and got to know the officers quite well. A few days out of here she was also sunk—I hope my friends are safe.

The news here is very good and everyone is high spirits and talking about home again. I would certainly like to read an American newspaper or hear an American broadcast. We did hear from London that a big coal strike was on in the States. If that is true, and I have no doubt it is, it's a hell-of-a thing. If some of those bastards were over here and doing without a lot of things—things that are needed so, I think they'd forget about strikes until the war is over. A good many Americans have had a bad time just because such things go on. We think it stinks.

Darling, it's very late and I must get some sleep. Goodnight, and I hope you can read this. It's written on the floor by candlelight. Give my love to Annie and R.L.

I love you, Darling,

Frank

❧ ❧

June 5 — Just as I started to write this note tonight two shells came over from close by. Didn't hit near us but I wonder what the hell is going on There is no air raid as yet. It's bad to get shot up by our own shells. On June 3rd, I was given a birthday party by the British Sisters and Officers and our American Nurses. I didn't know anything about it till the last minute and they came by and took me down to the cafe in the Village and we all had a fine time and an excellent dinner. The French people who own the cafe had a drink (toast) with us and then kissed me on both cheeks in true French style. I was even kissed by the cook, a nice old lady. After dinner we sat around and sang American and English songs and drank scotch and soda. In this British outfit we have good scotch and beer. Have had no mail in over two weeks.

June 9th Things are very quiet, not even any good air raids. Surgery has dropped off and we are just cooking in the heat. However, quite an event did happen today. I managed a bath. Tonight we are having a big hospital party.

❧ ❧

2nd Aux. Surg. Gp. A.P.O. 534 New York, N.Y.

June 14, 1943

By Post

My darling Margy—

                                          My Darling Margy

Today, after almost a month, I received 33 letters, most of which were from you. However, I heard from Gray, Parsons, Harkins, Mother, Ruth and Charlie Cliff's father. I had a wonderful time reading and rereading them. It was so good to have all those letters. This has really been a red-letter day in many respects. This afternoon I ate with Commander Lill on his ship and just listen to this — I had steak & french fries and birds-eye corn & apple pie. I had forgotten such food existed. In the ships mess the officers just sat and watched Mac (Capt. Ewing, my assistant) and I eat. They enjoyed it and were so damn nice to us. After dinner we took a nice hot & cold shower bath and then rested a while on a good soft bed. I could hardly retain myself. We heard American music and read American magazines only six weeks old. Be sure and save April 26th issue of Life for me. There is a very informative picture on page 20 if you know what I mean. From previous letters you possibly know what I was in and saw.

Anyway, to continue my story of today. While on the ship we had an air-raid and I had a grand stand seat on deck between the guns. It was a fine show with all the trimmings. Then again tonight we had an encore that was something. So much goes on around here that its like trying to watch a three ring circus.

You asked what I was C.O. of — it's a Detachment that I brought up by air. We came here first and then went to the front (p. 20.) Forsee is not with us and I think he is very glad not to be. Anyway, I've done worlds of surgery and have seen about everything there is to see. Again the fortune-teller was right in what I would see. It's a hell-of-a thing. So far I've been lucky in everything and am having a fine time for myself. Sweet, as for needing anything, all I need is you. Otherwise, I've learned to live without a lot of things I once thought were necessary, and it's not bad. I'm eating, sleeping, working, swimming, traveling and never have a dull moment. I really feel sorry for the ones back home missing all this. Of course, I'll be ready to come home but only when it's over. We often talk about home and stepping out for an evening in the bright lights and all.

*We expect to move soon but the above A.P.O. will be correct. I
believe it's the same as Ben's.*

*Sounds like you have had a wonderful time in Miami. Sure wish
I could be there with you. When I come home we must get around
lots. I'm afraid I have the wanderlust now and it will be hard to
control. One gets a new aspect of life here. A great many things are
not as important or as necessary as they used to be. However, I guess
we all can get back to the old routine. We'll have to catch up with
those in practice at home and I think we can. Sounds like Stover is
doing all right. Darling, I'm sorry I haven't given you a home and
the many other things I would like to have, but I didn't plan it this
way and I will do all those things some day. I'll always love you and
we will from now on always enjoy life and do everything we want to
do. Nothing much matters but loving you and being happy. In you I
have both.*

*Henry Harkins is writing another paper on our work. Would you
write him for some reprints?*

*This letter has gone on and on but somehow I want to keep
on writing — it will probably wear out some censor. Tell Gray I
appreciate his letters, I now have had three from him.*

Your guesses up to now have been correct. How do you do it?

*As soon as I get time to collect my pay for the past two months,
I'll send you a money order or cable it. Then when I meet you at the
boat be sure and bring the check book 'cause we are really going to
play a bit before going to work. I've got a lot of catching up to do.*

*Darling, I must go now — its very late. Thanks for all the letters
and kiss Annie and R.L. for me. I love you, dearest,*

Frank

June 15th Yesterday was quite a day. I received 33 letters from
home after receiving none for a month. It picked me up greatly.
My thumb is well and I can now use both hands to operate,
however I made out with one hand and a plucky red-headed nurse

                                           My Darling Margy

for 2 weeks. Yesterday afternoon I went down on the S.S. Morris and had dinner with Commander Lill. A good steak and french fries and corn and apple pie. One of the best meals I've ever eaten. Then had a shower bath (first in a good many weeks). After this we had an air raid while on the ship. I had a grand-stand view on the gun deck. Its noisy and rough. Last night after returning to the hospital at 10 p.m. we had a hell-of-a raid. One shell hit us but did no damage. We heard it coming and jumped into a ditch. Then again at 3 a.m. this morning we had a repeat. I was much too sleepy to bother and went on back to sleep. Seems like things may pick up for awhile. We hear from Hq. in Oran that the gang is having a fine time. They are living in tents but have a villa as a mess hall and Officer's Club with 12 French girls as waiters. They are on the beach and living the life of Riley. We must get back there for a brief period before the big show starts which will be soon. This heat here is getting bad. I operated this a.m. and lost about a gallon of sweat. It takes all of one's energy.

June 17, 1943 Ordered back to Base at Oran. Have been tearing down and packing yesterday and today. Last night the British gave us a party. It was a party to end all parties. Everyone had such a big time we are having an encore tonight. I'm afraid we have corrupted the British Army.

On the night of June 15th I spent the night on a British M.T.B. Boat. We had a big time and saw the air raid from a gunner's point of view.

Tomorrow we start back to Oran by way of beautiful Constantine by truck and train. God knows when we will get there. So long 'til Oran.

June 20, 1943 Arrived in Constantine two days ago and have been having a wonderful time. We traveled here by truck and it was rough. Ran into the British 8th Army and slowed down.

Constantine is the most beautiful and thrilling city I've seen in N. Africa. When you approach the city from the North the sight takes your breath. It's built on a cliff with a tremendous valley on both sides (east and west). In the center of the city there is a sheer drop of a thousand feet. This is spanned by several bridges and the views from them are unequalled. The city itself is beautiful and there are many people of all races here. Life is gay — and this approaches the glamour side of war. Totally different from our stay at the front. Last night the French Garrison here invited the Officers of E.B.S. Hq. where we are to a party and a dance at the Garrison. We went and had a very fine time. Many good things to eat and excellent French wine. I met many nice French officers and ladies. The ballroom opened onto a beautiful terrace overlooking the city. We ate in the ballroom and drank wine on the terrace 'til the wee hours this morning.

In two days I will take my detachment to Oran by French railroad. It will be some trip as I have a private car for our group. There will be about 50 of us. So long 'til Oran.

❧ ～ ☙

2nd Aux. Surg. Gp A.P.O. 534, N.Y., N.Y.
En-Route, June 24, 1943
By Post
Dearest Margy-
For a good many hours I've been on a very slow N. African French train. It is sort of a combination train, troops, freight, sheep, etc. I have a private car for my group and we are having a swell time despite the heat, dirt, food and lack of water. It keeps us busy day and night keeping the Arabs out of our car and holding on to our baggage. We live, eat, sleep in one coach. I've set up a mess unit in one end & latrine in the other. The food of course is all canned and cold. At intervals, when the train stops we get hot water from the engine and make coffee and shave. For sleeping we find places in seats & on the floor- nurses included. Our clothes haven't been off in some time and won't be for several more days. One distinct gripe on this train is that it is full of bed buggs and now they are all through

                                                    My Darling Margy

our baggage & bed rolls. We scatter insect powder & scratch- its great sport. During stops we find water here & there and chlorinate it in G.I. cans (garbage cans) about all I can say is that it is wet. Stops are many and speed is way slow. The coach is European style, that is, all compartments with an aisle down the side. We are traveling through a hot, dry part of Africa. All in all this train trip will be one of the high-lights of my Army days. A group living for days in a coach and getting a kick out of it. I'm in command and have a world of problems, eating, drinking water, sleeping and protection. At the moment our train has been sitting in this little Arab town for 4 hours and we were only to stay here a few minutes but that is the way the whole trip has been. I'm sure this will be a worn out bunch when we reach our destination and like-wise sure that no one will ever forget it.

I believe that this train is about to move again so I'll close and write again later.

Be sweet and take care of you for me. Give my love to all.
I love you, darling.
Frank

June 25, 1943 Left Constantine two days ago with four teams (9 officers, 6 nurses and 8 enlisted men) in a private car plus a baggage car. The coach is an old European type dirty car. It is full of bed bugs and now so are we. Travel is so very slow with many stops and layovers. We sleep on the seats and on the floor. I have made a mess unit in one end of the coach. Our food is "C" rations and nothing is cooked or hot, just eaten out of the cans. At this stage of the game everyone is worn out and exhausted and we are little better than half way. Water now is more of a problem than ever. So far I have managed to get enough at stops and chlorinate it for drinking.

We arrived in Algiers this morning at 8 a.m. It's now 4 p.m. and we are still waiting to move on to Oran. As I sit in the coach writing this the A.A. guns around the railroad yards are firing.

This coach rocks with every discharge of a gun. Haven't seen any planes yet and no bombs have fallen. If we get moving soon we may make Oran by tomorrow night and its only 187 miles. Fine service !! If you think it is easy to be in charge of a troop train, try it sometime.

June 28 — Arrived in Oran yesterday and was tired out. It was some trip. Our bivouac area is beautiful. It's on a beach just out of Oran. We have a villa and pavilion overlooking the blue Mediterranean. Swimming is wonderful and everything is perfect. This is still my rest period but will end in about another week when I go east again in the region of Bizerte for the invasion. What a show that will be. My luck holds and I'm going along.

This army is really "Snafu". I was ordered from between LaCalle and Bone to rejoin my unit at Oran and then retrace my steps to Bizerte or Mateur. Anyway I'm seeing Africa.

July 3rd After another train trip I arrived in Algiers again today, tired and dirty. Our bivouac is 14 miles east of Algiers but we spend our time in the city. Algiers is the largest and all around best city in N. Africa. Coming up on the train 22 French nurses and ambulance drivers came back to our coach and we had a very fine time. Of course the Col. was there making it official...almost!

July 5, 1943 Have been having a fine time in Algiers but, as everything else, it's just about over. In a day or so I'll take my team back to the Bizerte area for the invasion. I believe I'm going over in it. I have my assignment. My guess now is that the invasion will be on July 14th which gives us very little time to move up. The gang has gathered for a drink so I'll stop.

                                   My Darling Margy

2nd Aux.Surg. Gr. A.P.O. 534 NY, NY
July 6, 1943
By Post
My darling-

For the first time in a long time I'm sitting in a chair and writing on a table. This morning I had a nice cold bath and put on clean socks then we had a fairly good dinner just a few minutes ago. Now I'm at the Red Cross writing and relaxing. Darling if you ever have the chance do everything you can for the American Red Cross. They have been so nice to us and helped us out on many occasions- in fact they are the only organization that has done anything for us. This morning I ran into a medical officer from Camp Polk, a Lt. Anderson, you didn't know him. Col. Nicholson is here but I missed seeing him. I'm seeing more people in Africa from home than I ever dreamed I would. It's great fun.

In a few minutes several of us are going to take a trip through the Casbah (Casbah=Medina). I'll let you know if it is any different from my previous trip or did I tell you about it? Anyway I was entertained in a beautiful Arab home in a Casbah. I sat, ate, drank and talked with them. They had a twelve piece native orchestra playing for Capt. Moore and me. We had a night that I'll never forget and we are the envy of the outfit. Few Americans have been able to do this. There is lots more to tell you about it and I will but I can't write it. We'll see see what today's trip is like. Yesterday I went out to see my C.O. while I was with the British. He is here now and was glad to see me. I had tea with him!!!

I'm still having a big time in this city. There is so much to see and do. One never gets around to everything but I've done the high spots and how.

Did you ever receive the two money orders (in one letter)? I am keeping the stubs so let me know when and if you receive them. I'll send you more soon but at present I haven't had time to get paid. My last pay was for April. However I still have a few francs. When the Red Cross is around you don't need many francs. At this minute

I'm listening to "White Christmas" over the radio and it reminds me so much of you and Atlanta. Darling, I sure would would like to be with you in Atlanta now. I'd even love being at Camp Polk or Vicksburg and I never thought that would happen. However, I don't think it will be too long before we are home and together again. I've been over quite a time already- seems like ages.

I'll close now and take my trip- wish you could go along cause I know you would enjoy it. Good bye for now Sweetheart.
I love you dearly,
Frank.

⌒‿⌒

July 9th Arrived in Constantine this afternoon after a 36 hour train trip. We are being rushed to Bizerte for some reason, which probably means an invasion is about to come off. I'm leaving at 4:00 a.m. by truck for Bizerte. Our unit is dead tired but we will push on in a very few hours.

July 11th It's happened and we just made it here in time. I brought 4 teams to the hospital yesterday and went right to work. The invasion of Sicily began at dawn yesterday and things have been popping here since. Many planes are over us day and night and except for one occasion all have been American. The casualties are coming in but not as many as we had expected. From what we hear the invasion is going very well. The Bizerte area is certainly full of Americans and equipment. I was just up and met Col. Churchill, the surgical consultant for N.A. He gave most encouraging reports of the invasion. At present I'm in process of setting up four surgical teams and getting them into operation. This damn thing of being C.O. is a headache. No more time, will write again later.

July 19th I've been working (operating) day and night since the recent invasion. I'm doing most of the surgery at this hospital (114 Station Hosp.) even though they have 5 surgeons. However, these

                                    My Darling Margy

surgeons with the hospital are not very much and don't seem to care much for work. Its O.K. with me cause I get to do more.

I've acquired a little 5 yr. old Arab boy. He was in an accident yesterday and I amputated his right arm. Now I don't know who he belongs to and I guess will have to keep him which will be fine 'cause I've grown very fond of him. He is so little and cute and a perfect patient — never whimpers about anything. Had a very fine time on a party last night in Bizerte. When work lets up a bit I'm going over to Tunis for a day and look around. 186 bombers flew over us today and I hear went to Rome for a little hell raising.

2nd Aux. Surg. Gp. APO 534 New York, NY
July 19, 1943
V Mail
My darling Margy,
I've been so very busy, going most of the time. We've a big job on our hands, and I'm glad to say, doing it well. When I get home nothing will ever phase me. Yesterday I amputated the arm of a little 5-year-old Arab boy. He had been in an accident and was brought to me. He's a perfect patient and doing well, but I don't know who he belongs to or where he's from. I guess I'll just keep him with me when he recovers. I've grown very fond of him. He could shine my shoes and make my bed, etc. I'll just bring him home with me, OK?

The heat and dust continue on every day. I sent you money orders for a total of $134 and later wired you $125. Buy something you want with it and have good time for both of us. I have no use for money now. Activity continues here, and we see and hear a lot, and are getting used to it and good at ducking. Forsee has given me full rein and I'm running our show. It's quite a big one now, and it's running well and known to be working well. Sweetheart, I'm still in good health and haven't received the Purple Heart. Be a good soldier and remember me to all.

I love and adore you and miss you so. And write.
Frank

2nd Aux. Surg. Gp.
APO 534, New York, NY
July 21, 1943
V Mail
My darling,

I've just finished an all night job and am now on my cot trying to rest, but it's so damn hot that's impossible. It's 116 degrees in the shade and on occasions it gets much warmer. The nights are not cool any more, which of course is not so good, but it does get better when the sun goes down. The news continues very good, as you know. They can't stand much more.

Again, no mail in several days, but am looking for some tonight. Everyone over here seems to get regular mail but our outfit. That, of course, is due to our frequent moving. I live out of a val-pack and bedroll all the time, and am quite used to it now. Today I was able to have my clothes washed. Expect some clean ones tonight, and how I need them. My little Arab boy is doing fine, and so far still belongs to me. No one has come to claim him, and it seems OK with him. Another pay day comes up soon, and I still have my billfold full of last month's pay, so I'll wire you more money after the first. It takes about 2 weeks to get there. By the way, I've never received your cable.

Thanks a lot, dear, but I don't need anything. I'm doing fine and have the essentials. Keep your eye open for a nice light tan suit and white shoes. It will be swell to dress again.
I adore and love you, Darling
Frank.

2nd Aux. Surg. Gp. APO 534, New York, NY
July 22, 1943
V mail
My darling,

Last night I received several letters from you, Mother and one from Maynard. In all I got 15 letters and had one very fine time reading and re-reading them. Now I wonder how long it will be 'til

                    My Darling Margy

*I get mail again. Your letters sound so good and are very interesting
– especially the night you got drunk and stayed out. Guess I'll have
to report that to R.L. Anyway, you are lucky that you can get rum.
About all we have here is wine and foul beer. Haven't seen a drink of
bourbon since I've been out of the U.S. Sounds like things are going
damn well and I don't expect to stay out long. However, I've been
doing a tremendous amount of work here and really doing some good.
I've had two excellent assignments so far. By the way, did I tell you
I was train commander on one of my recent trips across Africa? Its
quite a job. I am now at the same spot I was in on May 8th which
was not Bone. The nights are now beautiful and not so active. The
cable hasn't come yet. I don't have much faith in them.*

    Be sweet, my darling cause I love you. All my love,
Frank

2nd Aux. Surg. Gp APO 534, New York, NY
July 25, 1943
V Mail
My Sweetheart,

    *Today I wrote you a long non-V mail letter. It's unusual and
you will get it before too long. Another patient of mine will drop you
a line when he returns. You may write him if you like—he will tell
you I am well and happy and working hard. Today is Sunday and I
haven't had so much to do and have even taken a nap this afternoon.
Living the life of Riley. Dear, everything is going well, and I am in
excellent condition. The food now is good, and about all I want and
can't get is an ice cold Coca Cola. I'll really make up for it some day.
Perhaps you had better start laying away a few for me. Could you
send me one? Today I had canned turkey for dinner and it was swell.
I am having excellent results with burns, and so far in this campaign
have lost very few. Also having excellent results with surgery and am
certainly learning a lot, and have learned that one can do a great
deal with very little. I guess my luck just won't wear out 'cause I've*

*My Darling Margy*45

certainly had it over here (more ways that one). Darling, write often, and think of me lots. Three letters from you today and one from Sarah. Give all my love.

I love you so,
Frank

July 26, 1943 Sicily is almost ours and probably will be completely taken this week. Of course the news today of the resignation of Mussolini was great but not unexpected here. Something is in the wind with Italy and I don't think it is invasion. Our work has been much lighter for the past 2-3 days and now we don't have a great deal to do.

We'll probably have a slump in a week or so 'til the next chapter begins. Tomorrow I'm going to Tunis for the day and probably do a little shopping. We have had no air raids in Bizerte this trip — too quiet. This afternoon I ran into Capt. Jennings, M.C. from Tampa. He is a patient in the hospital with malaria.

2nd Aux. Surg. Gp. APO 534, New York, NY
July 28, 1943
V Mail
My darling,

Last night when I returned I had two letters and the comb from you. It was so good to get them. Recently when I was in Tunis I had dinner with Milo Hoffman again. On that trip we also saw ancient Carthage. It was very interesting, and in its hey-day must have been quite a place. So you see I continue to be quite the traveling man, and am not missing much. Again, our work is light and we can get around. Today is a nice day with a breeze and quite comfortable for a change. My little Arab boy patient was taken away the other day. His father was found and he transferred him to a French hospital. I am broken hearted. I had planned on keeping him. Nothing else new has happened here in the past day or so, or rather, nothing I can write about. Things are looking so good I'll probably see you before you get

 My Darling Margy

*your degree—that's rather indefinite, isn't it? Darling, I think of you
so often and love you so very much. I'll always want you as I do now.
I adore you, Sweet.*
Frank

Aug. 3, 1943 All hell broke loose last night and today. To begin
with a group of 12 of us (officers and nurses) went in to Ferryville
last night for a birthday party for Maj. Taexler. We had a splendid
time but came in too late. About the time we came in, the guard
at the hospital gate was shot and the Col.'s jeep was stolen. All
of us were on the carpet today and my guns were taken until the
investigation is over. No one seems to know who shot the guard.
Its such a hell-of-a mess it's funny. Then today we were swamped
with wounded from Sicily. I've worked like the devil all day and
most of the night. I'm ready for the war to end. It really is hell.

*2nd Aux Surg Gp, APO 534 NY, NY
Aug 4, 1943
V Mail
My darling-
Just now, I got several letters from you and Mother. It was so
good to hear from you. Your letter of July 19th was so funny. You
just finding out about me in the Tunisian Campaign. Sweet, it was
really something and there were some tight spots. During that show
we were bombed in Bone, gunned in Bizerte and shelled west of
Tunis. Everything came out alright and I'm none the worse for it.
Please don't worry about me, I'll take care of myself and come back
to you, but as long as I'm over here I might as well see and do what
I can. After my rest, I spent a wonderful week in Algiers and had
such a fine time. It's a real city including the Casbah. I didn't make
the show in Sicily, others who were not in the Tunisian affair were
sent. I'll make the next. Lately I've been very busy— working most of
the time. Other than that there is not much to tell except that things*

are going well and I'm still getting a kick out of it, but I'll be glad to get home. Margy, you must get out more and have more fun. Don't forget how to have fun cause we are going to play and have a lot of it when I come home. I think we will play til the money runs out then I'll start to work. O.K. ? Darling I must run now, be sweet and I love you with all my heart. Til tomorrow,
Frank

Aug. 5, 1943 The guard shooting is cleared up and I understand I didn't do it. I got my guns back today.

Aug. 7, 1943 By Golly, we were bombed last night. The first we've had since my Bone days with the British. Our ship was sunk but not much damage done. Perhaps things will pick up and we won't be quite so bored.

Aug 8 — Had a nice day in Tunis today. Had dinner at Mon Village and champagne at the Belvedere. Tunis is a nice city, much more so than Bizerte. Work is slack at the moment. I'm ready to move again.

V.- MAIL No. 818268

To: Mrs. Marjorie Chunn
Landis Hall – Florida State College for Women.
Tallahassee, Fla.
U.S.A.

From: Maj. C. F. Chunn
2nd Aux. Surg. Gp.
A.P.O. 534, N.Y., N.Y.
Aug. 9, 1943

My darling- Today, I received several letters from you. The most

                                      My Darling Margy

recent was July 26th just after you had returned from Birmingham. I hope you had a nice visit and that traveling wasn't too bad. Sweet, I'm glad that you received the money orders and the cabled check. I had begun to think the M.O. was sunk. You must have miss-read my letter — I've never had my head shaved just clipped very close. On my most recent trip I had the finest sort of time in Tunis. Its a very nice city with many things of interest. We also had several bottles of excellent real French champagne. It was the last in stock and after much maneuvering we got it. I'll still say that it is the King of drinks. Margy, guess what!! Today I got a real bed to sleep on. After it was put up I tried to take a nap but couldn't sleep. It is very strange but I can't sleep on it – it's too comfortable. Guess I'll put my cot back up tonight. Its like an old friend. Funny things happen to one. What will I do when I get home? Bring two cots? Darling it was so good to hear from you today and I wish I could see you in black lace panties. Thinking about it just plain gets me down. So long for now and, Sweet, I love you and want you with all of my heart, Yours, Frank

Aug. 16. 1943 Work is going full blast again. Many wounded are pouring in from Sicily and I'm out on my feet tonight.

Had a rather extensive air raid last night. Today the unexploded bombs are being dug up. Margy, I wish you were with me tonight. I need you so, now, Darling. I'm blue and want you so. If I could only come across the miles to you tonight. Do you understand what my heart feels and is saying ?

Aug. 17, Sicily fell yesterday. We will probably hit Italy next and soon.

Aug. 18, 1943 Last night we had one hell-of-an air raid. We saw at least three shot down (Nazi), one in flames. It was beautiful but horrible. Guess we'll have lots from now on. The bombs were quite near and I've resumed hitting the ground.

Sept. 2 1943

Several of us went in to Ferryville last night to the French Naval Officers Club. There we met 4 British Naval Officers who invited us to their ship for a drink. We went to their ship which was a Destroyer and had scotch and gin. Had a very fine time and right in the shank of the evening we found ourselves targets as the Jerries were bombing the harbor. We went on deck and watched a first class show. No hits on us. Everything else remains about the same. I'm invited back on the Destroyer.

Sept. 15th

Things remain about the same, the weather hot and food bad. We've been on one package of cigarettes a week and they are Chelseas. The wind keeps everything covered with dust. I sweep my bed out with a broom before turning in at night. I've had a great deal of surgery to do since I've been here at Bizerte. Some of our teams are now in Italy and here I sit. I tried every way I know to be on that trip but the Col. decided I was needed more here — dammit and dammit.

The ship carrying 7 of our nurses to Italy was bombed and sunk off the coast of Italy. They were all saved but with some casualties. The ship, by the way, was a hospital ship plainly marked but she's on the bottom now. Seven British nurses and 15 British officers were killed. We've had several nights recently when German paratroopers were dropped in our area. It has made the Guards jumpy. A few nights ago I came in late and be damned if I wasn't shot at 4 times. If they keep that up some one may get hurt, but I don't believe this guard could hit the side of a barn. I'm so damn fed up on Africa and want to go to Europe. Think I will be soon.

Sept. 20 — Yesterday was Sunday and a gang of us went to the beach for a picnic and swim. Comdr. Tatterdale (Navy), a friend of mine, brought excellent fresh steaks and scotch. That was

My Darling Margy

absolutely the best steak I've ever tasted in my life. We cooked
them in real butter and while we were waiting on the meal had a
scotch or two. Work has slacked up a great deal. I want to leave
this damn hole of Africa. I think Europe would be swell — we'll
see.

Sept. 27, 1943

Yesterday the rains began and today we are in mud ankle
deep. Just like the old Bone days when we lived, slept and
operated in mud. I hate to think of going through another rain
season in Africa. It's such a damn mess. My bed last night was
wet and the blankets muddy. Today we were loaded down with
wounded from Italy. This bunch was really shot up. It's depressing
to see so many with such awful wounds. I'll have a good many
days of work getting these ready to go on back. The Col. said
today that we would be going on to Italy soon. I hope so, I'm fed
up with Africa. Had a chance to fly to Egypt for five days but the
work is too heavy. Certainly wish I could have gone. Some friends
of mine in a Fighter group here wanted me to go along. They
make this trip quite often, perhaps I can go later.

Oct. 24, 1943 Haven't written in this book in some time. I have
been very busy with surgery. The wounded have been pouring
in from Italy and we have had many motor accidents here. This
week I amputated three legs. They were all Americans and in bad
shape. Yesterday I got orders to pack and leave here on 10/26/43.
I understand we are going to Italy but will go to Algiers for
embarkation. That's fine 'cause Algiers is a nice city and a little
rest there will be fine. There is lots to do there. So long 'til Algiers
or Italy.

Oct. 27, 1943

My detachment returned to Headquarters yesterday and we
are just lying around and resting. It's a bit wet and muddy but I

understand we won't be here long. Sounds like we are on our way to Italy. I won't unpack. More teams are coming in today.

Nov. 5, 1943 This morning we went from Bizerte to Mateur by truck (in the rain) and then loaded on a French train. Everyone is very tired and when we lie down to sleep swarms of bed bugs attack us. By now we have bug powder over everything and us but it does little good. We have drawn rations for a 9 day trip and it's only 800 miles from here to Oran, our destination.

Nov. 9 — Tonight we arrived in Oran after a 4 day train trip. The trip wasn't so bad. We had fair food and wine and plenty of bed bugs and cold, wet weather. I haven't been out of my clothes since we left Bizerte and am a bit on the dirty side. The hell of the whole thing is that when we arrived we were sent direct to a staging area 20 miles out of Oran. We are now on a barren, cold and wet hill top. The tents leak and it's just one hell of a mess. Our food is "C" and "K" rations.

Nov. 16 1943 Have been having a good time around Oran and Sin-El-Turck. We come into town every day 'cause our camp is impossible. We have no heat, no water and lousy food. It's rained most of the time and everyone has colds. However, if one can stay in Oran it's not too bad. I hope to hell we get out of this place soon.

Nov. 18, 1943 Tonight everyone is happy. We loaded onto the Hosp. ship "Shamrock" and we are warm, dry and well fed for the first time in 2 weeks. This is a swell ship. I even had a hot shower tonight. We will leave tomorrow but you couldn't get a member of the 2nd Aux to leave this ship tonight. It's much too comfortable and warm and so different from the mud, cold and rain.

     My Darling Margy

Nov. 19 — The ship weighed anchor and left Oran this
afternoon. We are on our way to Naples. God be willing. The
weather is bad and sea rough. Many are already sea sick and in
their bunks. The ship is rolling and pitching quite a bit. Expect a
3 day trip.

Nov. 22, 1943
Our first 2 days were very rough and many were sea sick.
The third day at sea was nice and everyone came to meals again.
Again I'm a good sailor and haven't been sick.

This morning at 6:30 we passed quite close by the Isle of
Capri and Mt. Vesuvius and had a good look at both. Both
were very impressive. We then sailed into Naples harbor and
disembarked. Naples harbor is full of sunken and half-sunken
ships. The docks are blown up and things are a grand mess. At
present we are in a wrecked building on the outskirts of Naples.
Haven't seen much of the city as yet but will get around some
tomorrow. It certainly is swell not to see Arabs around. The
Italians seem glad to see us. The front lines are not far away and
Naples is frequently bombed. We shall have some fun.

Nov. 26th Have been having a wonderful time in Naples. It is a
very fine city despite its damage. The Via Roma (main drag) is
full of very fine and interesting shops and stores. Went to the San
Carlo opera and enjoyed it. Several of us shopped most of the day.
I bought a very beautiful cameo and several other things to send
to you, Margy. Also had my picture made.

Nov. 28th Today a gang of us went to Pompei and Vesuvius.
Pompei was so very interesting. We had a good guide and went
all through the place and saw so many interesting things. Pompei
must have been quite a place in its hey-day. Tonight when I came
in I found out that I'm leaving with my team in a day or so for
the front. Will be attached for the time being with the 38th Evac.

(Charlotte Unit). We'll see how the campaign goes.

2nd Aux Surg Gp, APO 534, NY NY
Nov. 28, 1943
V Mail

My darling wife-
I've had a busy two days looking over the city and area. I've seen some wonderful things here- many things that are very famous and historic. There is certainly a great deal to see and many places to go. However, I guess I'll move on shortly and go to work. I expect to see P. Sanger, etc soon. By the way, I saw Capt. Pain (Dr. Pain-Ford Hosp) a couple of days ago. It is still nice to run into friends from home. I wish that I could write you all about this place but the censor is very strict here and I can mention nothing that would locate me. You will just have to guess. I'm usually always forward. Sweetheart, I enjoy having this picture of you and look at it all the time. I had a photo made of me as I told you and will send it in the box with the other things. Hope it arrives O.K. I got you a very beautiful cameo and I certainly wish I could see you in the white silk thing I'm sending. Darling, be sweet and love me for I love and adore you with all my heart. I'll write again as soon as possible.
Goodnight my Sweet, I love you, so
Frank

Nov. 30th Arrived at 38th Evac. today. We are now right at the Front with the 5th Army and backing up the (left blank) th Division. The guns are very close by and shake the ground day and night. At night the sky is lit up with hundreds of flashes. We can stand in front of our tents and watch our shells hit on the mountains in front of us where the Jerries are. It's close but we can render a real service here by getting the wounded quickly.

Dec. 6th Well Christmas is not far off, but it won't mean much this year. So far, we have had rain and mud and the most mud I've seen. We even operate in rubber boots. Our tent floor is mud. In the mornings the water on the ground is frozen, then during the day it melts and gets soft and it's more mud. We have plenty of water now, but I wouldn't think of taking a bath in this cold. The work is damned heavy, and we are at it night and day. It is planned that we operate 8 hours and then rest but it's so heavy that I've just finished 16 hours at the operating table and then had to make Ward Rounds. 16 hours doesn't sound bad, but 16 hours of battle wound surgery will tire anybody. I've removed so many bullets and shell fragments that I do it in my sleep. It seems that these are the worst wounds I've seen.

We are set up in a mud field just south of Venafro and Pazzilli.

Dec. 10th

Had a daylight air raid this a.m. Several German planes flew very low over us and A.A. shells were all over the sky. We weren't hit but saw a plane knocked down. Surgery goes on without a let up. I'm on the day shift now, at first was on the night shift. Under field conditions surgery is done very differently. In our O.D.'s, we roll up our sleeves, wash our hands and arms in a pan of water, put on gloves and dive in. Surgery is very radical due to infection especially gas-gangrene developing.

Dec. 18th One more week 'til Christmas. I'm trying to get my rest period in Naples during Christmas. Naples and Sorrento are the only places we can go. Impossible to go any further north 'cause the Germans are right in front of us. Christmas in Naples will be fine, if possible. A shell hit near us two nights ago and thank God was a dud. The guns continue night and day and must be blasting the hell out of somebody. Seems like we will be going on into Rome before long now. The surgery goes on and we are living about the same. At least I have a stove in my tent now and managed to take a bath today. God, did I need it. Margy, I sent you a package today. It's your Christmas present but will be late. This is the first chance I've had to pack it. I love you, Darling.

Dec. 28, 1943 Last night I returned from a 3 day leave in Naples. I stayed at the Parco Hotel (Naples' best) and really had a very nice Christmas. Was invited to Humphrey Bogart's birthday party by him and enjoyed it. Perhaps I took just a bit too much to drink. Had a good turkey Christmas dinner and went to several parties. I slept in a bed, between sheets and had a hot bath everyday, something I haven't had in weeks. Also, I could dress in blouse and pinks and act like a gentleman again.

Jan. 1, 1944 — Happy New Year -
and what a New Year. For the past 3 days we have been rushed to death. The wounded have been pouring in much faster than we can take care of them. Last night at mid-night, I knocked off after operating 20 hours straight. The team had done double duty and were worn out. Went to the tent, had a drink for New Years and turned in. An hour later a hell-of-a rain, snow and wind storm came up and blew the hospital down. During the storm it was necessary for us to evacuate all of our patients during the storm. My tent blew down and everything I own including me got soaking wet. My Christmas packages were ruined and we were really "sad-sacks." This is one New Years I'll never forget.

Italy
January 2, 1944
V Mail

My Darling-
I haven't written you in several days- nor have I slept except for a few hours. A great deal has happened. Recently I spent 20 hours at

　　　　　　　　　　　　My Darling Margy

the operating table, working as fast as possible, one case after the other til we all were bushed. Then I went to my tent to sleep and a hell-of-a storm came up and blew the hospital down. My tent came down and I and everything in it got wet. This was during the night and it rained, snowed, and blew like hell. It was the damnest night I've ever seen. The mess tent blew away and all the food, we had none for some time. The patients had a rough time but we didn't lose a one and got them all out. We've been digging ourselves out of the wreckage and mud since. All my Xmas packages were ruined and our New Year's dinner lost. All in all it was quite an experience and a big mess. In eight hours after we were blown away, I was operating again and only today have I gotten any sleep. Now I'm feeling fine and none the worse. The weather now is very cold and I will never gripe again about Africa.

    Sweetheart, I hope you had a nice Christmas and New Years. My Xmas was fine but the New Year's will never be forgotten. I've missed you so and wanted you so very much.

I love and adore you,
Frank

Jan. 5, 1944- Having another wind storm and it's bitter cold. We are about to close the Hospital before it blows away again. However, as yet we are still operating and getting patients. For the past week I've been operating under the movie-camera, doing a series of wounds and operations for the Navy. Had a bit of an air raid today and got a very close look at German planes.

Jan. 7, 1944 — Work very slow for the past several days. The weather continues very cold and there is lots of mud. Don't guess I'll be in Italy long now. Sounds like another big show somewhere and I guess I'll be there. We have been for the past 6 weeks just behind Venafro. The artillery is here beside us and it's a damn noisy place at times.

Diary of Major Frank Chunn
Book Number Three

Jan. 10, 1944

The several days that I have not written in my diary may someday be explained but not now.

Anyway since writing last I've been called back to Hq's from the 38th in re' of a little beach party that will come off soon. I'm back at Hq's which is near Cacerta, Italy and am doing nothing but resting and drinking with the ole gang again.

Jan. 14,

A couple of days ago a group (4 teams) of us were packed off to a staging area out of Naples. We are again back in the rough, eating "C" rations and no bathing. We are getting ready for a landing somewhere and the indications are that it is going to be plenty rough. Our group is with the Combat Engineers and we go in on "D" day — where ???

Jan 19, 1944

This morning we were called early and sent to the point of embarkation -out of Naples- and are now on a British L.S.T. lying in the harbor. We are part of a large convoy and we are going places. I've been briefed, have my maps and know where we are going. (I won't write it down as yet.) I'm to lead a group ashore on "D" Day and give the first medical support for the coming invasion.

I've sent my money home and taken care of everything 'cause someone is bound to get it this time.

Jan. 20 — Still lying in the harbor waiting for the show to begin.

Jan. 21, 1944

This afternoon we got under way and now we are in a large convoy headed up the Italian coast toward Rome. There is no chance of a leak now. We will land in the morning at dawn on the beaches of Anzio and Nettuna, Italy, which is about 30 miles from Rome. We understand it will be plenty rough. My orders are to lead my group across the beach (once we are landed) to a spot marked x on the map and to dig in. Everyone is in excellent spirits tonight — The U.S.T. Captain gave me a couple of drinks of scotch — guess he thinks it may be our last.

Margy, I'm glad you know nothing of this. I've an idea that Jan. 22, 1944, will live forever in my memory. We shall see — Goodnight and I hope not goodbye.

Jan. 22, 1944 — "D" Day at Anzio and Nettuna. I was up at 4 A.M., our convoy was approaching its destination and we had several things to do before dawn. Out on deck we could see the flashes from the naval guns shelling hell out of the beach. As dawn came we were ready and no one in my outfit seemed afraid. It was a very strange feeling that I cannot describe. Anyway with the dawn came air raids on the convoy while it was disembarking troops. I was given an O.K. for landing by our U.S.T. Captain. We climbed into the landing boat and as we did a large mine sweeper next to us was blown up and sank in about 5 minutes. Our landing boat headed for shore a mile away while the A.A. guns tried to cover us from every air craft that were raising plenty of hell. We landed at Red Beach just as planned and pulled in beside an U.C.I. A sand bar kept us out several yards so we backed out and landed 50 yards down the beach. This was the luckiest move of my life, because just as we climbed out of the landing boat onto the pontoon three Jerry planes came down the beach bombing and strafing. A bomb hit the U.C.I. where we had been 5 minutes before killing 8 and wounding 12. The U.C.I. burned and exploded. The remaining bombs fell to our other

                                    My Darling Margy

side and as yet none of us were hurt. The pontoon that we again climbed onto was slippery with blood and large chunks of human flesh and meat were scattered about presenting a sight that I'll never forget and I'm a surgeon used to such butchery. To go on, we dashed across the beach but not before 2 more strafings from Jerry. At this time we were, burning up, wet, tired but went on. I didn't need my maps 'cause I knew perfectly every mark on it. We went up the beach to a road, hoping that we would step on no mines. We reached our objective in about an hour after two more bombings and strafings. Artillery shells were landing lower on the beach and did not catch us. Finally we reached a spot that I knew was it (according to the map) and in a very few minutes every man had a nice deep fox hole. By this time I had seen six dead and about 12 wounded. I could do nothing 'cause I had nothing. My equipment hadn't been landed and we were the first medical men on the beach. I was with the 33rd Field Hospital which was still out in the harbor on an U.S.T. I did what I could with only a packet full of morphine. My men were tired, hungry and uncertain as to what would happen — so was I. Anyway later in day our equipment came ashore after having a casualty in our group, and we rapidly set up an operating tent, just off the beach. Our operating tent is set up and I'm now ready to start. I'll never forget this day. So long, I've a job to do.

Jan. 24, 1944

It is now about noon and I've just waked up. Until about 6 hours ago I've been operating since we got our tent up. We were the first to receive wounded and are the only ones on the beach that can give any surgical care. We are and have been swamped with patients, operating on them just as fast as possible. Our supplies are running out and still more patients arrive every hour. I'm doing major abdominal operations in my shirt sleeves with just a pair of rubber gloves on — there is nothing else to do. Half the time we operate in our helmets and it's trying to stay off the floor while operating. Jerry is really trying to push us into the sea and the air raids come about every hour. They are after the beach and we are 500 yards off the water. Everyone sleeps either in or next to a fox hole — what little sleep there is to be had.

The Artillery is right next to us and are blazing away day and night. It's truly hell on the patients and not so good on us. Last night our water point was shelled and we have none except for surgery.

I amputated a Col.'s leg and when he reacted from the anesthetic and asked for a drink, I had to tell him that we had none. As yet I haven't taken off my clothes since landing — they are muddy, bloody and look like hell. Now we are operating about 18 to 20 hours and resting 4 to 6 hours. The food is about gone and what we have had is only "C" rations. Supplies have not been landed as yet because we badly need guns, men and ammunition if we are not to be pushed out.

However, if this does happen the group will cut cards and the two low men will stay with the patients. We had hoped to evacuate most of our patients but we hear the hospital ship was bombed and sunk during the morning. So long, I must go to work.

Jan. 28 -

We are still at the same spot (on Nettuna beach) and continue to be bombed day and night. Bill Lees was hit on the head with a large shell fragment during a raid this morning. His helmet stopped it and he is only shaken up. Milt Tinsley was hit in the chest with a 20 mm bullet. Bas operated on him and Tinsley will be O.K. but was evacuated back to Naples.

Our first real tragedy has come. Johnny Adams and his enlisted man McComb were lost when the British hospital ship was sunk a few nights ago. Johnny was last seen going below deck to get the patients out and the ship sank a few minutes later. He was not picked up.

                                    My Darling Margy

The surgery is heavy and it's a grind to keep going. Our beach head is still very much in doubt.

Margy, at times like these, I think of you and look at your picture and thank God that you are safe. I love you so much and don't know whether I'll see you again or not.

Our nurses arrived today and are helping out so much.

Jan. 30, 1944

Everyone is dead tired. It's been eight days of a nightmare and last night was very bad. A heavy German air raid hit a Cruiser and a Liberty ship in the harbor here where we are. One ship was beached in front of us and then blew up. It rocked us out of bed. A few minutes later the other one blew up. Both are burning now. This has been a costly invasion, but we are holding our own and advancing some. I have a touch of the flu, but feel better today and am back on the job after 12 hours in bed.

Jan. 31 — We moved today from the 2nd Platoon to the 3rd Platoon which is inland a way. Wounded are pouring in and we have come up to take care of them. With me are Fishwick, Easley, Hoeffding, Moore, Lynch and Lallich. We moved in at 4 P.M. and began operating at 6 P.M. — not bad.

However, at this spot we are well within enemy artillery range and their shells are now passing over us hitting Anzio and the beach.

We stay on the ground of the operating tent about as much as we are up. When a shell whistles over one just can't stay off the ground. It's a hell of a sound.

We are so close that we can hear the gun fire, the shell whistle and then explode — it's not good !!

Feb. 2, Today, I've been a Major a year and had planned to celebrate, but can't find time — perhaps tomorrow.

Today, I had my first bath since leaving Naples 2 weeks ago

and changed clothes that I've been wearing since I left the 38th Evac. over a month ago. It's a grand feeling to be clean again.

I understand we move up again soon. I'm ready to relax in Rome.

Feb. 4, 1944

Things are slacking up some. Jerry is still throwing artillery shells around us but so far they have only been close — no hits on us. Nettuna and Anzio which are next to us catch hell daily. The food is really lousy. We've been eating "C" rations and hard tack since "D" Day. A nice steak and piece of real bread would be fine. A few days ago, I operated on a pretty little 3 year old Italian girl who had been shot through the rectum. She is so cute and doing all right. I would like to bring her home but I guess I can't. No mail since leaving Naples.

Feb. 5th

German artillery have been shelling us regularly for the past 18 hours. The 2nd Platoon of the 33rd Field, which we left a few days ago, was shelled out and have just pulled in. They were about a mile away from us and I doubt if they are any better off.

The shells are sailing over us now. I can stand in front of my tent and see the German lines. They are not far away and they are still trying to push us into the sea. The British on our left flank were pushed back 3 miles today and we received about 100 wounded. We can't spare many 3 miles. About an hour ago I went into Nettuna to see a friend in Signal Corps. We went down into a full wine cellar that they had taken over. In this cellar are about 3500 to 4000 gals. of fine Italian white wine. I'm offered all I can take and so put 50 gals. on the truck and brought it back with me. There is a fortune in wine there if we only had it home — and it's there for the taking. There is much more wine about than food.

Nettuna was a nice little town but like everything else now

                                        My Darling Margy

is wrecked and being shelled. This is quite a situation, shells hitting all around us, flak coming through the tent, and air raids everywhere. Last night two German tanks came down the road shooting things up a bit and got away with it. Many strange things happen in this business. Still no mail -

Feb. 8th The deal gets rougher and the past 24 hours has been hell. Yesterday was a beautiful day and surgery was light. Then at 3:30 p.m. while I was operating, four German planes strafed and bombed our hospital (33rd Field Hospital) and the 95th Evac. which is set up some 15 yards. from us. Two bombs hit the 95th square and we were riddled. Bomb fragments tore great holes in the operating tent on both sides of my table and not a damn one of my team was hit including the patient. However, one of Capt. Hurt's boys was hit along with many others. The poor 95th Evac. had 25 killed and 48 severely wounded. We operated on all of them as we could still function. I'll never forget that bombing — the tremendous explosions and fragments coming through that tent like an express train. God was on my side that moment, but can it keep up.

Then when we were getting the mess cleaned up, the dead carried away and wounded patched up, we were shelled by 88's and that has continued and is going on right now. A big German gun that is hidden out here in the woods gives it to us every night. It is a 170 mm gun and really throws them in. We have given him the nick-name of "Lonesome Polecat". The shell scream suggests that. ?

Three American nurses and one girl Red Cross worker were killed. I watched 2 of them die on the table and could do nothing. We have had many officers and soldiers die last night but when you see our American girls shot to hell and in front of you something happens.

We are holding a beach head varying from 3 to 8 miles, all of which is under shell fire to say nothing of air raids. Three

hospitals have been shot up including us. One hospital ship has
been sunk and another hit, both loaded with wounded that we
sent them. My nurse was on the St. David that was sunk off
Anzio the night of Jan. 24 (Night of D-2). She was in the water
an hour before being picked up and taken to Naples.

The nurses joined us day before yesterday and now I don't
know whether to evacuate them to Naples or not. They won't go
and we need them so but no woman should be here. Our tents are
full of holes from bombs, shells and flak and no one knows when
they may get it. I hope if mine comes it's complete — I can't be a
cripple.

Again, may I repeat, that the American nurses I've seen and
worked with have more guts than a lot of men I know.

An hour ago, while operating on a G.I. under a local
anesthetic and during a shelling, I had a soldier put my helmet
on the patient. He looked up with a grateful expression and said
"Major, you wear the helmet; you are more important than I am."
We can't lose with soldiers and nurses like these, but it is costing a
price. I don't know what will happen tonight. I go back to surgery
at 8:00 P.M.

However, I do have one bright star from the recent mess.
A man from the 95th Evac. was brought in, I did a major
abdominal operation on him and operated on his popliteal fossa
(Kure negroir) where the artery had been torn. The leg was lifeless
and no circulation present. It was felt that an amputation (thigh)
would be necessary and that would probably have killed him.
Anyway I sutured the popliteal artery under a flashlight and this
morning the leg and foot have good circulation and will be saved.
The patient is in fairly good condition. This happens only rarely.
During the operation it was necessary to give him 2000 cc of
blood and 500 cc of plasma. I transfused him again today.

This whole thing is a bit on the rough side. Oh yes, I forgot to
mention — the ass end of my truck was shot off yesterday.

                                    My Darling Margy

Feb. 11, 1944

Last afternoon at 5:30 P.M. we were shelled with German 88's. Our outfit (33rd Field Hosp.) was directly hit four times. Two of our nurses were killed and 5 officers and 3 men hit and wounded. The hell was knocked out of us. Our tents were riddled and most of those not in fox holes were hit. We started patching up our wounded under shell fire and later taking care of our dead. I got our nurses in a fox hole and then went to the ward to see my patients. The poor devils — I put them on the floor and covered them as best as possible then the wounded started coming in, and we put on bandages, gave morphine and blood transfusions while lying in the ground and hoping to hell that a shell would not hit the tent. Tony Erwin, Phil Giddings, and Capt. Block were hit. Two nurses were killed with the second salvo. As the shelling began, I dashed into our nurses' tent and found two of them naked and taking a bath. They were rushed to a fox hole with only a coat, helmet and boots and thank God we got them there. In the past four days, seven nurses have been killed and God knows how many men. The 95th Evac. has been evacuated back to Naples, and we are taking on the load.

At this stage of the game, we are thinking of when it will come to us. We understand that the German Army has been ordered to push us off this beach head and into the sea by tomorrow. We shall see what happens tonight. Everyone has dug fox holes, deep and wide and I guess it's a good idea. This entire area is under shell fire and we could be knocked off any time.

At this moment a spot about 1000 yards away is catching hell from the Artillery and we are now wondering if it will come here again. Our 3rd Platoon was knocked out last night: the 95th was knocked out and is now gone. We got it but are still in operation, for how long I don't know. Its quite a deal———

Feb. 12th

Another shelling and a bombing this morning. The shells

were close but we didn't get hit this time. However, we did spend an hour in fox holes and were damn glad to be there. The nurses (some of them) are about worn out and so are the officers. Our blood supply is about gone and no more has come in. We will be in a jam if some doesn't arrive soon. Had white bread today, the first since the Invasion.

Now, it seems that it is only a matter of time 'til we stop a shell or bomb fragment. The 2nd AUXs have had a high casualty rate in the past three weeks. Emmi, Giddings were evacuated today with the Purple Heart Post-humous. So far this unit (33rd Field Hospital) has had 2 nurses killed, 4 officers wounded and 6 E.M. wounded. The 95th Evac. or what was left of it was shipped back to Naples yesterday and the 15th Evac. has arrived — they are ready to go back already——-

Feb. 13th

This is our 22nd day on the Beach head and we have no more ground than we had on "D" Day. The hell has kept up and this morning we have more of us wounded. Last night, while trying to cook some bacon (that I stole) in my tent we got it again. A rather prolonged air raid came off and a stick of bombs hit us square. The nearest hit was 20 yards from my fox hole. It knocked the hell out of us and the tents were riddled. Anyone in any of the tents would have gotten it. It just so happened that we had evacuated all of our patients and we were in fox holes. However, two nurses and 9 men were hit, one nurse rather badly. My team is still intact but now we wonder how long it will be 'til our time comes. Oh yes, after the raid our old friend "Lonesome Polecat" lobbed a few shells in but didn't hit anything. This morning we had another raid and were lucky again. Just after this many of our bombers came over and blasted hell out of Jerry. We could stand outside and watch the whole show. One of our bombers got hit and we watched it fall not far from us. Two of its occupants got out in chutes. I guess the others didn't make it.

                                      My Darling Margy

This has been and still is quite a deal — Don't know what the outcome will be but it doesn't look good now and 22 days of this is making some very nervous and jumpy. Now, at the moment, we are resting a bit and waiting for what the night holds.

Feb. 19, 1944

Several days since I've written in this book and it seems like months. I've lost track of time and now have no idea what today is. I'm sure it's the 19th of Feb. for the reasons I will relate. On Feb. 14th we moved up again and as usual are right at the front. I stand in front of my tent and watch the battle rage. We can see and hear, only too close, the machine guns and machine pistols of Jerry. Our artillery is in front and behind us — shooting over us. Anyway we moved up and immediately dug in. I'm sleeping 4 ft. below the ground and wish it were 10.

On the 16th the Germans launched an attack at the sector. It was one hell-of-a night. We stayed in fox holes during an entire night of bombing and shelling. They hit all around us but this time missed the hospital.

It's quite an ordeal sitting in a fox hole sweating out a bombing or shelling. This was the night of Feb. 15th. On the 16th (when the ground attack started) we received over 90 wounded (two other surgeons and myself). I began operating at once and did so for 26 hours. At the end of this period I hardly knew what I was doing — the team was out on its feet. We crawled into our holes and slept 5 hours and then operated again for 24 hours. The last stretch ended last night at 8:00 p.m. and I slept 'til 10:00 a.m. today. All patients have been operated on and as yet I've lost none of mine. Its amazing what they can take. For example, on one lad, I closed a large sucking wound of the chest, explored his abdomen and resected some small intestine, amputated his left thigh, amputated two right toes, and debrieded 4 wounds of back and flank. Today, three days later, he is doing very well and I believe will make the grade.

At night we operate with the patients on a litter, then during the bombings we lower the litter to the ground and lie down beside the patient. We may be in any stage of the operation but its much better to have a live team and patient than dead ones.

This is something I thought could never exist and I don't know whether we will or not but we'll carry on 'til we don't.

I have as a patient (I may have mentioned this before) a beautiful Italian girl — lovely brown eyes, dark hair and most kissable lips — aged 3 yrs. I operated on her on the beach on D-1. She was shot through the rectum by the Germans and her mother was carried off by the Germans. She is with her father, a young Italian, and now both are very much attached to me and I to them.

Her father does my laundry, works about my tent and just does everything for me. Little Alberta is doing fine and today I carried her out in the sunshine. In a few days I shall operate on her again and close her colostomy. Then she will be as good as new and if she continues — in about 15 years will be a knock-out, a Glamour Girl.

In Africa, I wanted to keep the little Arab boy for whom I had amputated a forearm — now I want to keep the little Italian girl — wouldn't I have a strange family ?

Feb. 24th Nothing much new. We've been shelled several times during the day, but no hits — just too close for comfort. This afternoon I operated on a soldier who had been shot through the liver, right lung and heart. He lived to reach the operating room but died during the operation. I don't understand why or how he lived that long.

Feb. 25th

More shelling today, but no hits. It's raining and cold and I've only written letters today. I'm off call for 12 hours and am taking it easy. There has been very little surgery for the past 12 hours.

Hope it continues.

Feb. 29, 1944

This has been a hell-of-a night and day. We've been shelled almost constantly during this time. We received direct hits and had several wounded and one killed.

I had to operate during part of the shelling and it's no fun standing at the table then.

In a big hurry we evacuated all of our patients and we will evacuate in the a.m. Probably we'll have quite a night in fox holes.

This is an unusual one: last night I operated on a soldier and did the following — (1) Sutured a hole in the stomach (laparotomy), (2) Amputated right thigh, (3) Amputated right arm, (4) Amputated half of the left hand, (5) Dorsal laminectomy, (6) Debrieded fragment wounds of both arms, right shoulder, several wounds of the back and a large one of the buttock. He is still living and in fair condition and was evacuated today with the others. This move will probably kill some of the patients but if we stay here God only knows what will happen. —It's rough.

March 1, 1944

Moved today and are now set up about 3 miles back. Haven't been shelled as yet but this looks like "Bomber Run" to me.

March 2, I was right, last night we had a severe air-raid. No direct hits on us but they were too damn close. Two ships were hit and burned in the harbor.

March 6 -

Have been kept busy at this new location, but haven't been hit by anything as yet. Three fresh teams arrived yesterday but went to 93 Evac. Had snow and hail yesterday and its cold today. No bombing for past 2 nights but tonight is clear and I guess Jerry will be over.

About a week ago, a friend of mine gave me a 300 gal. barrel of white wine. I was unable to move it when we moved, so I took all I could, gave as much away as I could and then poured 100 gals. on the ground. I almost cried but it had to be done.

C'est La Guerre

March 8, 1944 Another bombing last night and it was damn close but again no hits on us. I was operating at the time — a most uncomfortable feeling at the operating table. We have been unable to land food and supplies for a few days, due to shellings and bad weather, and we are back on "C" rations and hard crackers. Shells continue to hit all around us as this whole damn beach head is under enemy gun range and has been since we landed. It gets tiresome after 48 days.

March 22, 1944

During the early morning (3:00 a.m.) we again were heavily shelled by German 88's. Result — 9 killed and 11 wounded. The 15th Evac. Hosp. which is beside us got a hit in a ward tent. The 56 Evac. and 52 Med. Bn. also had one casualty each. The shelling lasted about 20 minutes at an average of one shell every 5 seconds and were zero'd in on our area. To me was an intentional shelling and again disastrous. Again thank God for a nice fox hole — it has saved me many times.

We have now been on this beach head 61 days and have had 61 days of this sort of stuff. The 94th Evac. Hosp. landed today and are setting up. They should lighten our load a lot and perhaps we will go places. Last night several of us sort of hung one on — something to do in trying to forget.

March 23, 1944

A great deal of shelling around us. Nettuna and Anzio (behind us) are almost constantly under shell fire. Of course the

                                        My Darling Margy

whole damn beachhead is under German range. Something has
got to happen.

March 28th

March is about over and still the weather is cold and the
mountains are covered with snow (Sunny Italy!)

Last afternoon we had a heavy German day light, air raid. I've
never heard quite so much noise in my life. Several of our group
were hit with "flak" but no damage was done this time. During
the raid I was operating, doing a thoraco-abdominal and couldn't
duck — it's a damn uncomfortable feeling and not conducive to
good surgery.

Again about midnight the Artillery threw shells in and hit
a gas dump close by. We were lighted up like a birthday cake.
Otherwise, a quiet night.

March 29th

Tonight at 9:00 p.m. the hospital area was again worked over
by German bombers. We received two sticks of bombs as direct
hits. As a result 5 killed and many wounded. Hopkins, Gay,
Shorbe and Bas were wounded but not seriously. A close friend
of mine Capt. Hoffman of the 93rd Evac. (which is 50 yds. from
us) received a severe leg wound and may lose his leg. A hell-of-a
night.

March 30-

Today we began digging the hospital in for sure. The
operating tents will be set down in the ground as will the ward
tents. This should help a great deal.

April 3, 1944

Last night was a heavy one. I operated all night. We were
shelled all night and well into the morning. Another gasoline
dump close by was hit and burned hours. At about 3:00 a.m. we

had a heavy air raid but were not hit. I climbed out of my fox hole at 2:00 p.m. and will go on duty at eight. We have been unable to evacuate patients for several days and now are about filled up. The nurses are being sent back to Naples for a rest period and God knows they need it.

We've still made no headway on this beach head.
4:00 p.m. were just shelled by a German 210mm gun. The 56 Evac. next to us was hit twice and a cook killed. The shells made craters 6 feet deep and 10 feet wide. Its a hell-of-a gun.

April 4, 1944 We have been heavily shelled for past two days and today received two direct hits from our friend the 210mm gun. Luckily no one was hurt. The thing that saves us is the very soft ground. The shells bury themselves before exploding and knock a large hole in the ground.

April 5th
Heavy shelling has continued to hit us for past 3 days and it's no damn fun. We eat in shifts now so that everyone won't get killed if the mess tent is hit. Everyone is dug in as best possible.

April 6th Still it continues. A shell hit 3 yds. behind Sullivan's tent this a.m. and tore a large hole in the ground. Caved in Sullivan's fox hole but again no one hurt here. The 56 Evac. also hit at same time — one killed and one had both legs blown off. Its really a rough season.

April 9, 1944 (Easter)
This is my second Easter overseas. Last year I was in Rabat. Today the 38th Evac. Hosp. arrived to replace the 56th Evac. The poor old 56th has been knocked out. They have not been hit as much as we but they are whipped in spirit and it's good they are going back. I hope the 38th come through O.K. I went over and saw all of the old gang. Tonight sounds like another shelling

beginning. I write later-

April 15th

Still on Anzio but nothing much happening. The usual
shelling and air raids but we haven't been hit recently. Work has
slacked up some.

April 21, 1944

Had a rather prolonged air raid last night and a small day
light raid this afternoon. Last night the beach head was dive-
bombed but the hospital was left alone.

May 3, 1944

Haven't written in this in a good many days. Nothing of great
importance has happened. The beach head has been fairly quiet
for 2-3 weeks. Last night we had two air raids and some shelling.
The 38th Evac., which is not far away, had two shell hits last
night. No one was hurt but the X-ray table is a mess. This is their
first and I guess they aren't happy.

Received our first beer ration today — 3 bottles and it was
fine. We may start for Rome soon and will I be glad to get there.

May 20, 1944

As I start to write, after so many days, the air raid warning is
sounded. It's still day light and Jerry is starting early tonight.

We are just before something big and we hope it comes out in
our favor. We hope to see Rome soon.

Since I last wrote in this diary, not a great deal has happened.
Just the usual shellings and bombings, not hitting us. It's overcast
and tonight should be lively.

May 23, 1944

A new attack started this morning from the beach head.
I understand that we have taken Cisterna but don't know any

further news. The wounded started pouring in at about 8 o'clock (a.m.). I'm working nights for the next 4 nights and expect to be very busy. I was very busy yesterday. Six more teams arrived here and will probably get all they want.

Last night Jerry dropped tin-foil strips all over us attempting to jam the radar. We had many of our bombers come over this a.m. to burn the pants off Jerry.

We shall see what happens in the next few days —.

May 26, 1944

I moved today with the 1st Platoon up to Front just behind Cori. We passed through Cisterna, completely in ruins. It is the most bombed and shelled town I've ever seen. Much worse than Bizerte or Anzio.

May 29, 1944 Since arriving here I've done nothing but operate. We've had many casualties and have been busy as the devil. I've had very little rest. We've just cleaned up the last case and will probably go forward again in a couple of days.

June 3, 1944 (My birthday, age 32)

Today we left Cori and are now set up in a fresh battle field near Carraceto. The dead are still lying around and the place is covered with German and American guns, tanks and other equipment. The smell of the dead is strong and nauseating at times. Again we are in a red poppy field that is pock marked with shell and bomb holes. We are ready to operate and have just received our first patient, a German, shot through the chest. Don't expect to stay here long. Looking forward to seeing Rome.

June 5, 1944 The Platoon is moving up today, this time to Rome. We've waited a long time for this deal and now we are going. We've started packing and expect to see Rome by tonight. I think that I'll do a little celebrating the first chance I get. So long 'til Rome.

                                        My Darling Margy

June 6, 1944 We've just gotten the great News on the radio. The
Invasion of W. Europe has begun and I guess it's quite a show.
I had hoped to be in on it but I guess I couldn't expect to make
them all —

I drove into Rome yesterday and have never seen anything
like it. All of the Romans were out on the street welcoming us,
giving us drinks and seemed very happy to see us. Everything is
wide open, the stores are well stocked and Rome has not been
damaged.

While I was driving down the main drag a battle broke out
between snipers in a building and us on the street. It was a wild
turmoil and quite a scene. However, when the Americans turned
a couple of .50 cal. machine guns on the building the snipers were
quickly taken care of. Several American soldiers were wounded
and Maj. Betts and I went into the building with .45 in hand to
take care of them. After this we drove around the streets of Rome
and visited some bars and cafe's. It was like a world gone mad
and far outstripped Ferryville and Tunis when they fell. I'm going
back into the city today to see some of the famous places. I saw
the hell-raising yesterday.

I bought excellent Asti Spumante champagne for $2.00 a
bottle, the best cognac I've ever tasted for $5.00 a bottle.

June 7, 1944 This morning as I got up we watched about 700 to
800 of our Liberator bombers fly over and seemingly they were
headed for southern France. Perhaps we'll see France yet.

June 8, 1944 No work today. I took a grand tour of Rome and
saw it all. I went through St. Peter's (Vatican City) and truly
I've never in my life seen anything like it. I went through the
catacombs of St. Callixtus and visited a cave in which the
Germans shot 520 Italians.

We are in camp at a nice spot between Rome and Lido — about 5 miles out of Rome toward the beach.

June 9th Moved today — 40 miles North of Rome and set up just north of Civitavecchia on the coast. As usual the place was blown apart. I saw two of the big rail way guns that the Germans used on us at Anzio. The barrel was 70 feet long and the col. 12 inches. Its the biggest gun I've ever seen.

June 11th Moving up again today, I understand about 40 to 50 miles, and will work tonight. We're really moving up Italy and seeing a great many new and interesting places. It's difficult to keep contact with the enemy as he has certainly been on the move. A great deal of German equipment has been left behind. Had a beer ration last night and for a change no air raid. Another Purple Heart was given to our unit 4 days ago. (Cpt. Thomas — hit in chest — doing O.K.)

June 12, 1944

I'm now 75 miles North of Rome. We are set up in a field and operating. The clearing station is here with us and the Front just around the corner. Expect to move up again tomorrow.

I received a pint of whiskey and a Coca-Cola from Margy today, an unusual treat. Thank you, My Darling.

June 14, 1944 — I was relieved today for a rest and am now in Rome. We arrived at dinner time after long, hot, dusty trip by truck. Our bivouac is in the park of Vatican City, a very beautiful place on top of a hill with many tall pine trees and palms. Will get around Rome some more tomorrow. It's very nice to be resting with no air raids or shelling.

June 15th Spent the day looking around Rome and even visited several nice bars. Rome is quite a city, full of people. The city has not been bombed except for the rail way station. As usual the Germans have looted the stores and shops and not very much is left.

Sunday, June 18, 1944

I visited St. Peter's again today and then went through the Sistine Chapel of the Vatican. It's the most beautiful thing in Vatican City. At noon I had an audience with the Pope. He blessed two rosaries for me. I'll send them to you Margy. Otherwise I'm still resting.

June 28, 1944

I've just finished a 3 day leave at the Excelsior Hotel in Rome (one of Rome's best) and had quite a time. (Baths, clean sheets, clean clothes, excellent food, dances, etc.) Now I'm more tired than when I went on leave. Will have to get back to the front for a rest.

July 1, 1944 We moved up to Piombino, Italy, today by motor convoy and am now in bivouac in the field. Life is very quiet.

July 2, 1944. I operated all day today at the 56 Evac. Hosp. My team was called in for today only due to an emergency. The 56th was swamped with wounded and needed help.

Fishwick and I have asked to go on the new invasion that is coming up.

July 13, 1944 The invasion group of the 2nd Aux, which includes me, boarded a Liberty ship at Piombino today bound for the staging area around Naples.

July 17, 1944 Arrived in Naples after a 4 day trip. It was one hell-of-a trip. The ship was dirty and the weather hot. On the way down we saw Elba, the Isle of Monte Cristo, then by the Isle of

Capri and Ischia into Naples harbor.

Naples is much cleaner and nicer than when I last saw it six months ago.

July 20, 1944 At the moment I'm with the 11th Field Hospital in a staging area at Sparanise, Italy (above Naples).

Two days ago our group was asked for two volunteers to make the Invasion with the Paratroops. I thought it would be interesting and Fishwick and I asked to go. We had no competition. As yet it is unsettled but I think it will come through. Margy, I know you wouldn't like this but I couldn't, somehow, pass it up and then on the other hand someone has to do it. The call was for a good surgeon because we will be completely isolated 'til the beach head troops fight through to us and I think I can fill the order.

Yesterday I visited Cassino and Monte Cassino and what was left of the Abbey. I was at Cassino front in Dec. 1943 but never saw it til yesterday. Cassino is the most ruined city I've seen yet and I've seen a fair number.

We have a few days left in which to complete our packing, etc. The job coming up sounds like a big one, I hope this is our last.

July 24, 1944

I saw Col. Forsee today. He asked me about the para troop deal and seemed surprised when I said I still wanted to go. He promised to let me know definitely within a couple of days. If I go Fishwick will go along and that will be a good deal. I went swimming today and think I'll get tight tonight.

July 26th The Col. sent me word that the Paratroop deal was off, said I was not expendable enough.

However, I will land with the 36 Infantry Division on "D" Day. I wish I knew where but I guess I have a good idea—

My Darling Margy

August 4, 1944

We have been staging in a hot, dusty field about 14 miles north of Naples for about 2 weeks. Everything has been packed — even our tents and bedding rolls. We've been sleeping on the ground under a tree. I got fed up with this and so for the past 4 days have been living in a swell six room (two baths) apartment in Naples. I'll stay here a few more days and then go back to the field. My guess is before long we will be in Southern France and that the Normandy landing will be minor compared to this one. This will probably be my last web-foot job in Europe.

Aug. 10, 1944

We boarded the troop ship General George O. Squiers today at Naples and are ready to start on the Invasion of Southern France. On ship-board the quarters and food are good. Otherwise no news.

Aug 11, 1944

Pulled out into the harbor today and just waiting for the convoy to get going —-

Aug. 13, 1944 -

We left Naples this afternoon in the Invasion Convoy headed for Southern France. I know where we are going and what to expect and it's going to be a honey. So far the voyage has been uneventful and nice. We sleep in our clothes tonight.

Aug 14, 1944

Tomorrow is "D" Day for us in So. France. We are now in convoy rapidly approaching our destination (? destiny) and will land in the morning on the beach near St. Raphael, France.

I was just out on deck and see the battleships have joined us. Tonight will probably be lively and tomorrow the works —.

Aug. 15, 1944

We landed today on Green Beach at St. Raphael, France, after a terrific Naval and Air bombardment. It was truly something to see. Massive battleships firing broadside into the beaches and German positions and great flights of bombers dropping bombs. However, we had our losses but not heavy.

Tonight the beach was raided by Jerry planes and one ship was hit and burned.

Aug 17, 1944

I worked all night last night with the 56th Med. Bn. clearing station. We had many cases. By the way, I did the first case of major surgery in the St. Raphael beach head sector (a soldier shot through the small bowel, large bowel and liver).

Today, I moved up with a platoon of the 11th Field Hospital to above Frejus and am now about 15 miles inland and expect to move up again soon. The roads are loaded with the Americans going north and the Germans going south under guard. The way we are rolling this thing can't last long.

France is beautiful, the people nice and very glad to see us.

Had a close call last night when a bomb fell near our villa on the Riviera.

Must go to work — will write more later-

Aug. 19, 1944

The unit is set up at Le Muy but only for a short stand. The lines are moving north fast.

Aug 20, Today we moved up to Draguignan and it's the same old story. The people are happy that we are here and everyone is having a fine holiday except us. We are quite busy.

Aug 21, Last night someone threw a grenade at Geo. Donaghy
and me while we were walking home (to camp) from
Draguignan. No one got hurt as far as I know but we didn't
linger long.

Had dinner with a very nice French Family.

Today moved up 95 miles and are now north of Valonne.
Expect to move again tomorrow toward Lyon.

Aug. 23, 1944

Moved up to Crest today and are set up and ready to take
patients. We had a 100 mile ride through a very beautiful part of
France.

Aug. 24, 1944

Last night Fishwick, Donaghy and I had a fine time in Crest.
We had drinks and dinner at a little French Cafe'. Met many nice
people and ate and drank with them. Also we were the guests of
the Macquis. (The Macquis are the French civilian army of the
Interior.)

Sept. 2, 1944

Moved up to Lafayette today. Only one surgical case,
otherwise just playing and looking around.

Sept. 5 -

Moved up to Bourg today. Quite a city. Had some good
French food and champagne.

Sept. 7, 1944

On up to Poligny in foul weather. Stayed in a swell little
French hotel in town and had an excellent time. I'll never forget
Poligny.

Sept 9,

Moved to Guingey today and expect to move on north in a couple of days. We are moving fast and really don't have much time to do much work.

Sept 11, 1944 Moved north 40 miles today and are set up and ready for work. Don't know the name of the little town next to us. Will probably move up again in one or two days. All of France that we've seen has been beautiful. We've had good French bread, cheese, butter and milk. The eau-de-vie is as mean as hell (even worse than corn whiskey). (Fretigney)

Sept. 16, 1944

Moved up again today, through Vesaul and 10 miles north of this city. Hospital is set up and ready for work. Looks like rain.

Sept. 18, 1944

It has been raining for two days and the hospital is now flooded. There is a foot of water in the operating, shock and ward tents. My feet haven't been dry or warm in two days. We are preparing to move to high ground today.

Sept. 20, 1944 Moved up again today through Luxeiul to Plombieres. We are right at the front and as usual are receiving patients. The artillery is damn close at this point.

Sept. 21

Was in Luxeiul today. Had a fine steak dinner and drank Kirsh for the first time. It's about as bad as eau-de-vie.

Sept. 25, 1944

Today, I finished operating at 3 p.m., loaded on a truck in the rain and mud and moved up through Remiremont to Elayes. The weather is foul and everyone is wet and cold. The platoon is set

   My Darling Margy

up and we are ready for work. For the first time we are living in a building.

Sept. 26, 1944 Had a fine sleep last night but was wakened by shelling (88's). The shock tent was riddled and there were several near misses but as yet no one hit. The shelling has ceased for the time being but I guess it will start again any moment. Sort of like the old days at Anzio.

We are drawing straws this morning for 3 day leaves in Paris. I'm keeping my fingers crossed.

Oct. 2, 1944 Since last writing in this book, I've worked night and day with a few hours sleep now and then. I've operated on an average of 16-18 hours daily for past 4 days. Today, I had my first shave in 4 days. There have been many wounded and we've had all we could do. Two days ago, I had an extremely interesting case as follows.

An American soldier was shot in the left flank by a shell fragment. X-ray revealed the fragment in the left chest, probably in the heart. I resected the 10th rib, left, and removed a shell fragment 2x2x1/2 cm. from the left ventricle of the heart, sutured the heart and pericardium. Then incised the diaphragm, removed the spleen (perf.) sutured two large holes in the stomach, exteriorized splenic flexure of colon (two perf's of) and drained the left kidney (perf. of). Today, two days later the patient is in good condition — T99.2, P114, R24, B.P.120/80. During the operation he was given 4000 cc of blood.

By the way, The Paris trip was called off due to the increase of work.

Oct. 4, 1944

Last night at 6 p.m. I left the operating tent after 19 1/2 hours of continuous surgery. I was so worn out that I was numb. I went to my room to go to bed and one of the boys pulled out a bottle of real American rye whiskey. We haven't had any in months so I got tight and stayed up half the night. Today I feel fine.

Yesterday, I anastomosed a Popliteal artery of a G.I. and he has circulation of his leg. He is doing fine and I believe that I'll save his leg. I've done this with success once before and I haven't known of it being done before over here. My heart case is living and doing fair.

Yesterday's total was as follows. Two laparatomies, one abdomo-perineal anastomases of rectum and Sigmoid, one thorocotomy, one thoroco-abdominal and an anastomosis of a Popliteal artery. I call that a large day's work.

Had an incidental air raid last night.

～

Oct. 20, 1944
France
By Post
My Darling-

Last night I received 4 letters from you and one from R.L. That was my first mail in days.

Recently, I've been very busy, working most of the time. I've been unable to bathe or even write. I'm shaving every third day and sleep when I can.

Do you remember me mentioning the soldier that I removed the shell from his heart among other things? Several days ago, I evacuated him to the Rear in excellent condition. He was sitting up and eating a full Army diet. That case has become famous here and I'm so glad that I could save him. For many minutes on the operating table it was either way and with the odds against him. After removing the fragment, I plugged the hole in the heart by inserting my finger and suturing around it.

In the past two days, I've resected the pancreas on three patients — lost one and saved two. Last night I had a soldier with the duodenum, stomach, colon, liver and gall bladder perforated. Today

 My Darling Margy

he looks fine and is coming along O.K. It's so good to see them recover and know that they will be well again.

No, my Sweet, I didn't turn down a chance to come home. I haven't had a chance. I was talking about something else. A surgeon was wanted for a certain job on "D" day and I asked for it. Now don't get upset, I'm just fine and working hard.

Darling, do what you like about buying a car. I think you should have one, especially for your teaching .

Not much else to write about. For a change the weather is nice today. I worked 'til 4 a.m., slept 'til noon and back on the job after lunch. I've about beat the team down but somehow I feel fine and had much rather operate than loaf.

Angel, I'm so glad you enjoyed your stay at the beach and that you like your new job of teaching. I'll sit in on one of your classes one day. Shall I bring the teacher an apple?

Be sweet, my love, I'll write again soon. I love and adore you and want you so,

Frank.

P.S. Did you receive the red roses?

Oct. 22, 1944 Work has continued heavy and no unusual news. We've had a couple of night air raids recently but they didn't amount to much. This a.m. at 0300 hours, I turned over a command car that I was driving. Burbank was with me and neither of us were hurt. The car is a total wreck and I don't see how we got out of it, but we did.

Nov. 6, 1944

I was just looking over the records and was amazed to find the following. During the month of Oct. 1944 four other surgeons and myself did 178 major operations (Thorocotomies, Laparotomies, thoraco-abdominals or amputations). We gave 958 bottles of blood (each bottle contains 500 c.c. blood). This was an average of 2,700 c.c. blood per patient. Of course some patients received more and some less than this amount.

For the past 3-4 days surgery has fallen off.

Tomorrow is Nov. 7. I guess Roosevelt will be elected again.

Nov. 10, 1944

Moved up with the platoon to Bryenes and set up in the French Civil Hospital. This is our best set up yet.

I looked over my cases today — the ones done in France since Aug. 15,1944, and find the following results.

Type of case	No. operations	Deaths
Cranial	2	1
Thoracotomy	13	1
Laparotomy	43	8
Thoraco-abdominal	15	4
Upper extremity	4	0
Lower extremity	8	0
others	10	0

Amount of Blood used = 322 bottles or 161,000 c.c.
Amount of Plasma used 100 units or 25,000 c.c.
This blood and plasma was given pre-operatively and during surgery, only.

Work is very slack for the moment. I haven't operated in 3 days.

Nov. 26, 1944

Moved up to Ban-de-Lanaline and set the hospital up in an old factory. I'm living in a room at the home of a nice French family. The artillery is all around us and it's about impossible to sleep. Work is heavy and we are short short handed. We are breaking in two new surgical teams from the 1st Aux. Surg. Gp. They are fresh from the States and have seen no forward, battle surgery.

                                          My Darling Margy

Nov. 29th I've shaved and brushed my teeth once in the past three days. We've had a full load of surgery and I've been going most of the time. I've been working with my team for 16 hours during the day and then helping the new teams the remaining hours. We only have two 2nd Aux. teams now and it's tough going. In one minute I'm going to take a stiff drink and crawl into my sack.

Dec. 2, 1944 I moved up to St. Marie today. Patients (6) were waiting when I arrived. Will stop now and go to work.

Dec. 12, 1944

For the past 10 days I've been so very busy. Capt. Jergesen and I have been doing all the surgery of the 36th Division and it has just about beat us down. Jergesen only does orthopedics so I'm doing all the chests and abdomens. I've been operating day and night. Twenty-four hours ago we stopped receiving patients and we'll move up again in a couple of days. Probably to Selestat.

Dec. 23, 1944

Moved up Ribeauville today and we and the 3rd Division Clearing Station are set up in a large, old building in town.

As we approached the outskirts of Ribeauville coming in our convoy was stopped. Only one truck allowed to dash in every 15 to 20 minutes because the road and town are under German observation and artillery fire. We didn't care to have all the personnel and trucks shot-up together. I came on in with the first truck and located quarters for my gang. Nothing happened.

Dec. 25, 1944 Christmas day and we are very busy. Operated all last night, slept a few hours this morning and have been working since. We had an excellent Christmas dinner this evening.

The Germans have been very active since we arrived. Many

shells have hit about the town.

Tonight at 7 p.m. a call came in for volunteers (surgical teams) to go with an Airbourne invasion. I asked to go and now have orders to report for duty in the morning. I think that this will be plenty rough.

Dec. 26, 1944. I finished operating at 5:00 a.m. this morning — then packed, drove to 2nd Aux. Hqs. and reported for the Airbourne job. I was told that it had been called off and that I wouldn't be needed and to report back to my post at Ribeauville. I got back at 3 p.m. and started operating again but with a fresh team as mine are out on their feet and I sent them to bed. It is now 10 P.M., I'm through and am going to bed. As best I can remember I've been operating and traveling for past 48 hours.

Dec. 27, 1944 Still busy and have a ward full of post-operative patients. This afternoon an order came in to prepare to evacuate as the tactical situation is grave. All unused equipment and baggage was packed and sent back to St. Marie today and we are to be ready to evacuate on a moment's notice. I've many patients too sick to move: guess I'll hang around with them.

Jan. 3, 1945

At last — I begin a two week leave in the morning. I'll drive back to Hqs. at Sarnebourg and then have two weeks to do nothing but rest, play and perhaps go to Paris. Today, I put Mary, my nurse, and Berby (E.M.) in the hospital. Both are quite ill. They will be evacuated in the morning.

Jan. 4, 1945

Damn everything. I arrived in Sarrebourg today (Hqs) after an all day trip and was promptly sent to the 116th Evac. Hosp. to be Chief of Surgery. Their chief is sick and the Hospital is loaded down with wounded — and I thought I was going on leave !!! To

                                             My Darling Margy

make things worse, Capt. Massengill and Sgt. Radowich, on my team, were sent to the hospital today — ill. Geo. Donaghy and I are the only ones left of the team. We started work at the 116th Evac. today. This is a new hospital having just come overseas and they know nothing about battle surgery. I'm taking all the major cases and trying to direct the rest. There are 85 operations here now to do.

Jan. 11, 1945

At last I'm finished with the 116th Evac. Everything is cleaned up and I left there today. I've just returned to Hqs. and thought I might get in a short leave anyway but hell no, I was given a fresh surgical team and will go back to the field tomorrow. I'm going north of Strasbourg 17 km., up into "the pocket", to the 57th Field Hospital. I understand it's quite a hot spot. Well, I'll have a little party tonight with the boys and call that my leave. This leave turned out to be a farce.

Jan. 12, 1945

Arrived at the 57th Field hospital just out of Boumath, Alsace, today. It's very cold with snow and ice over everything. However, we are in a building and it's not so bad.

Ready for work as usual — with a new team.

Jan. 16, 1945.

Have been busy since arriving here and the new team is working out fine. My old team (except Geo. Donaghy) is still laid up and I hear that Mary, my nurse, is being sent home due to her illness. I'm sorry but I'm glad she's going home. She's done more than her part in the past 2 years.

I guess I worked the team too hard and too long without a rest but here again we were needed and someone has got to do it. Don't know how long George can hold up but I think I can carry on O.K. Had a very tough night last night, and an attack began today so we'll be busy again tonight.

Jan. 19, 1945 — 7:00p.m.

Orders just arrived that we are to evacuate all nurses and all possible patients tonight. Jerry has broken through a short distance from us and the situation is grave.

As usual we have patients that cannot be moved, so a holding team will be left behind in the morning to take care of the non-transportable post-operatives with a few hospital supplies, food and medicine. And again as usual, I took the job. I'm evacuating my team but keeping my two enlisted men on purely volunteer basis on their part. We'll sweat it out and see what happens.

10:00 p.m.

All nurses and patients that could travel have just been evacuated. I have about 15 patients left and we shall remain. The Clearing Company evacuated two hours ago and we're alone now.
Jan. 20, 1945 1:00a.m.

More orders just arrived and the situation is evidently worse. I'm now ordered to evacuate all patients and equipment, me and my boys at dawn. Looks like I may not get caught this time.

Noon

I've just arrived at Saverne (Zabern) lock, stock and barrel and safe. We are setting up in a fine building with running hot and cold water, steam heat and electric lights. This can't last long. I expect to go back up into the "Pocket" at Baumath soon.

Jan. 30, 1945 Still in Saverne and have been moderately busy. However, orders arrived tonight for me to take my team back into the "Pocket" at Baumath. I'll leave in the morning and keep my fingers crossed.

Saverne has been very nice while it lasted.

                              My Darling Margy

Jan. 31, 1945

Arrived here in Baumath this afternoon and was supposed to meet the 11th Field Hospital here. Nothing is here except the Clearing Station. I have with me two American surgical teams and one French team. We are sitting in an ice cold building with no heat and no lights and as yet no Field Hospital has shown up — and by the way no food and have had none all day.

Feb. 1, 1945

Last night I borrowed one stove and six candles and 15 blankets from the Clearing Co. In one big room all of us slept — as follows, one French nurse, three American nurses, two French officers and nine American officers. We were hungry and cold. This a.m. the Field Hospital arrived and I've been operating all day. Its now 11:00 p.m. and I'm going to bed. It's been a very bad day. Jerry is raising hell here, we have no heat and I lost two patients on the operating table today. At this point I'm feeling very low — God damn low — the only bright thing is news of the Russian Advance.

This month I celebrate two years of this sort of thing. It's a hell of a way to make a living —.

Feb. 14, 1945

Last night while I was driving through Baumath in my truck the town was shelled and hole knocked in my rear tire. We got out of town on the double without further damage but it was a tight few minutes.

Feb. 28, 1945

Overseas two years today — it seems more like ten.

March 13, 1945

Today, I operated on a French soldier (F.F.I.) and removed a bullet from the heart, right ventricle. So far he is doing well.

March 14, 1945

Before dawn tomorrow the big attack starts — this time to push on into Germany and end this thing, I hope.

March 17, 1945

The push came off on the 15th and I've been as busy as hell since. We finished operating a bit ago — have a hospital full of wounded (very seriously). Will continue in action during the night and will move up in the morning close to the Rhine. Things seem to be going well but it's costing a price.

In two years of battle surgery, I've never seen so many soldiers with legs blown off as I did on March 15th. Our division got into a mine field and it was hell. Will write again after we move up. Back to tents and mud this time.

March 19, 1945

Moved up to Drachenbroom, France today and we are set up right in the Maginot Line. Our artillery is behind us and fires over us while we work.

We arrived at this spot at 1600 hours and received many wounded at the same time. Due to a shortage of trucks and an error, the X-ray unit and surgical equipment were four hours away. There was no possible way to evacuate these patients and also there was no blood.

I had my surgical instruments with me. I borrowed 10 sterile towels, some sterile sponges, several cans of ether, had some of the boys draw blood from everybody I could find and started operating on a litter. We stripped to the waist, washed our hands and arms and with four towels as drapes, I did a laparotomy — resected the right colon and terminal ileum. Following this I did a right thoraco-abdominal.

At about 2100 hours our equipment arrived. Capt. Barnett and I were the only two surgical teams along, so both operated

                                    My Darling Margy

continuously until 2000 hours of March 21, 1945. On that day relief arrived and we went to bed. I think I shall never forget my stay in the Maginot Line.

March 22, 1945

A volunteer team was called for today to go with an Airbourne Division on a jump into Germany. Somehow, I had no trouble in getting the job and am leaving tonight to join this unit. I have a completely new team with the exception of Burbridge (one of my enlisted men) who asked to go with me. The others are Capt. Art Adams, Capt. Herb Moore and Sgt. Williams.

March 23, 1945 -

What a hell-of-night and day. Last night I drove 5 hours to report to Hqs. and pick up my new team. I received my secret orders and was reporting to the Airborne when the whole damned deal was called off and I was ordered back to the 11th Field in the Maginot Line. After driving all day I'm back and about as bushed as I've ever been.

March 26, 1945

Moved up again today to Klingermunster, Germany, passed through the Siegfried Line and am now set up on the edge of that line.

Again we are moving very rapidly and having quite a time. One notices very quickly that these Germans are certainly no friends of ours.

March 30, 1945

Moved up to Gallheim, Germany, today and joined the 4th Division for the push through Germany.

March 31, 1945

Crossed the Rhine today with the 4th Division. We crossed

at Worms and moved with a tank and infantry column to a spot about half way through Germany and expect to move on up at any moment.

—— ——

Germany
April 1, 1945
V Mail
Happy Easter My Darling,
For the next one I will be with you and it will be a most happy one for me. This is my third Easter overseas and I hope never to be away from you for another. I am moving very fast these days and have seen quite a little bit of this country. Things are much different. We have absolutely nothing to do with the people(civilians). And every house we come to has a white flag hanging on it. There is nothing to buy and nothing that one would want. Anyway, I am getting along fine and am certainly glad that we are at last raising hell in this country. It is worth all of the waiting and "sweating".

Your new dresses sound wonderful and I wish that I could be there to see you and take you out wearing them. I would wear my new jacket and we would have quite a time for ourselves. I am back in tents and living the old way again and moving rapidly.

Be sweet, my angel, and write often. I love and adore you and want you so. Always your
Frank.

April 1, 1945 Easter and Mother's birthday. We're still waiting orders to move again. From the indications we are going to move through Germany much in the manner of a rat-race.

A German jet-propulsion plane just passed over —- about the fastest thing I ever saw.

April 14, 1945

A lot has happened in the past two weeks. Until April 9th I was with the platoon at Wurzburg, Germany. From that time until now, I'll just enclose this copy of my official report.

                                    My Darling Margy

GENERAL SURGICAL TEAM NO. 18
2ND AUXILIARY SURGICAL GROUP (DETACHMENT)
APO #887

12 April 1945

SUBJECT: Report of General Surgical Team No. 18, 2nd
Auxiliary Surgical Group (Det).

TO   : Commanding Officer, 2nd Auxiliary Surgical
Group (Det), APO 887, U. S. Army.

General Surgical Team No. 18 was placed on TD
with VI Corps on 9 April 1945.
For the assignment the team consisted of the following
personnel:

MAJOR CHARLES F. CHUNN,   O-448722, MC,
CAPTAIN WILLIAM F. ROSE,   O-492228, MC,
CAPTAIN WILLIAM H. CAVE,   O-268178, MC,
Tec 4 Lester M. Goodwin,   32387701, MD,
Pvt Lynn L. Burbridge,   16099610, MD.

The team reported to the Surgeon of VI Corps at
Mosbach, Germany and was immediately taken to the
airfield and put aboard L-5 planes and given instructions
for parachuting if it became necessary. At about 1800
hours on 9 April, 1945 the team plus surgical instruments
only, took off in six planes, heading for Crailsheim,
Germany to give surgical care to two combat teams of the
10th Armored Division who had been cut off by the enemy
for two or three days.

After about 30 minutes plane trip the planes landed
on the air strip at Crailsheim in heavy enemy mortar fire.

Major Chunn received a penetrating mortar fragment
wound of the right hand. Several soldiers at the air strip
were wounded and one transport plane was "knocked out"
by mortar fire.

Personnel and instruments were collected and the team was taken by jeep to the 80th Clearing Station of the 10th Armored Division which was in the basement of a building in Crailsheim.

About 35 wounded American soldiers were then at the station. In this group of wounded there were two patients with perforating wounds of the abdomen, four patients with penetrating or perforating wounds of the chest, two of which had a tension pneumo-hemothorax of two days duration. The remaining wounded consisted of extremity wounds with the exception of one penetrating wound of the head.

The operating room was immediately set up and the two patients with tension pnemo-hemothorax were treated, by relieving the tension, aspirating the chest and the giving of plasma. Whole blood was not present. However, three Baxter blood transfusion bottles were found in the clearing station and 1500 c.c. of blood was drawn from soldier donor's. 500 c.c. of blood was given to one chest case, and 1000 c.c. of blood given to one abdominal case who was in extreme shock. The remaining shock therapy was done with plasma. During the night two exploratory laparotomies were done, the two chest patients were treated. All other wounded were treated with penicillin, plasma if necessary, splints and dressings. No other surgery was attempted that night due to the absence of blood, sterile dressings, oxygen, and very poor light. Surgical gowns and drapes were exhausted on the first operation.

During the night the town was under constant enemy shell fire and straffing. The building was hit at least once.

On 10 April 1945 at about 1400 hours, 40 bottles of whole blood arrived. Total patient admissions to this date

Official report of mission behind enemy lines, Crailsheim, Germany, April 1945.

were 53.

At this time all patients were evacuated, including the post-operatives as there were no facilities for post operative care. One abdominal and one chest case died post-operative. Remaining were evacuated in good condition.

At 1700 hours, 10 April 1945, a soldier was brought in with a perforating wound of the abdomen. He was treated for shock and prepared for surgery. The patient was given ether anesthesia and was being draped when an immediate evacuation order arrived. The patients wounds were dressed and when reacted to anesthesia, was evacuated to a field hospital.

The clearing station and surgical team rapidly packed and at 1900 hours, evacuated Crailsheim in half-tracks of the last combat team to leave the town. The column's front and rear were protected with tanks and the evacuation was carried out under cover of American artillery barrage in orderly fashion. As far as is known two half-tracks and one truck were lost.

The evacuation terminated at 0400 hours 11 April 1945, some 30 miles west of Crailsheim. During this entire interval surgical team 18 was active in surgery, shock therapy, post-operative treatment, the evacuation of patients and the evacuation of Crailsheim, Germany.

CHARLES F. CHUNN
Major, Med. Corps,
OC, Gen Surg Team No. 18

April 18, 1945

Arrived in Paris today on leave and am staying at the Hotel Crillon on the Place de la Concord. It's truly quite a city and I anticipate a fine time in the next few days. Now for a hot bath, dress up and see the city.

April 20, 1945
France
By Post
My Darling Margy,

I am having the time of my life and certainly wish you were here. I've never seen anything like it. It's so unusual, gay and exciting that it's mad. I've seen things that I've always heard and read about and I'm living in the best hotel in the city. It's on that famous main drag [Champs Elysees]. I've always heard about it in April and every word of it is true.

It certainly was worth all the hell to get this leave, however, I wouldn't recommend getting shot to obtain a leave. I am enclosing a few memos of last night's rounds. We had great fun.

Sweet, I am getting along fine and am about well. I was so lucky not to have gotten it any worse. In a few days I will return to my job and be on hand for the "wind up" but at the moment I am living like a king and enjoying every moment of it. I'll really have to tell you about this episode.

Well Angel, I'll close and get around a bit- wish you were coming along but we will do this together some time.

I miss you and love you with all my heart.
Forever yours,
Frank
P.S. I've been recommended for another decoration.

April 22, 1945

My leave ends today and I've had quite a time. Paris is
by far the best I've seen since leaving the States. I think I saw
everything, went to most of the shows, night clubs and all-in-all
had a wonderful time. Sorry it had to end.

❧ ❧

April 22, 1945
France
By Post
Darling-
Today my leave ends and I start back to the front. It's quite a
distance from here and I'll have to travel the first part by train and
the last part by motor. I don't look forward to the trip but the leave
was well worth it. George Donaghy, Bob Dozier(my team) and I
have had a wonderful time. This is a gay, beautiful city- the lights
are on at night and everything in full swing. The first lights I've seen
since leaving the States. However, it's the same old story- there is
absolutely nothing worthwhile in the stores to buy. Champagne is $15
a bottle, a sandwich in a night club is $5, etc. In Germany we get
champagne, etc. for nothing (?)
I'm getting along fine and my wound is healing nicely. I'll be
ready for work in a day or two.
It is now more than two weeks since my last little job, so I guess I
can write something about it. (censorship regulations)
At about this time, somewhere in Germany, a certain outfit got
cut off by the enemy and were in a tight spot with no medical care.
A volunteer surgical team was called for to go into this place by air
and take care of the wounded. Somehow, I managed to get the job.
We took off in cub planes, flew over the battle line, and it was quite
a sight, and landed in a field which was under heavy enemy mortar
fire. While getting my team and instruments together, I was wounded
in the rt. hand by a mortar fragment. At first I thought that I would
be unable to operate, but my fingers worked alright without too much
pain.

We went to the cellar of a building and opened shop for business of which there was plenty. The town was under constant fire and our building was hit several times. My supplies were extremely limited and many things I didn't have, but during the night, I did two exploratory laparotomies, two chest cases and one severe knee joint. The other cases were treated with dressings, plasma, splints, and penicillin.

The town could not be held, so the next night, my patients, team, and I evacuated in the last armored column to leave. We had an American artillery barrage to cover us on the break out.

It was quite an experience and two days later I had my hand taken care of in an Evac. Hosp. However, I did take penicillin during our stay there which did prevent any gross infection. Now it is just about well and I guess that I'm none the worse for it.

Then I was given this leave and have had a wonderful time, but it's just about over now. Well, Angel-puss, the news is very good and I guess it won't be too long before "I'll Be Seeing You".

All my love is yours for always. I adore you and want you so much.
Forever your
Frank
P.S. Give Annie and R.L. my love.

April 25 -

Of all the damn luck! While returning from leave, I turned up with jaundice and am now in the hospital as a patient. Guess Paris was too much for me. However, I'm feeling fine now and expect to return to work in a few days.

May 8, 1945
V-E Day —- thank God ———

   My Darling Margy

May 10, 1945
Germany
By Post
My Sweetheart-

Last night I had a letter from you and you certainly are a curious little chicken.

Now I'll try and answer some of your questions, however, in recent letters I'm sure I've answered many. You were almost perfect in your guesses as to when I entered Germany and crossed the Rhine. No, I didn't get wounded crossing the Rhine. As you know by now it was on landing during an Airborne operation in Germany. Yes, I had a nice Opel car but lost it when I went on the Airborne. I didn't get it at the Opel plant and I don't even know where that is.

The busy period I mentioned was on our drive into and thru Germany. We were moving so fast and had so many patients that it was operate and move forward and we would have to leave someone behind on every move to take care of the post-operatives. We were strung very thin at times and at one time two of us (teams) took care of three Divisions. At this stand we operated 65 hours at one clip. It did look a bit impossible at times but we did it and no one went without proper surgical care.

Looking back on it, now that it's all over, I wonder how it was done but when the pressure is on a great deal can be done.

At present, I'm just resting and seeing Germany at my leisure. Our work here is finished. I'm living in a nice apartment, sleep as late as I like in the mornings, am having good food and a good time. We have a couple of Germans to keep house for us so about all I have to do is dress myself and eat — great life, isn't it?

I now have six bronze battle stars, one Arrow-head, almost five over-seas stripes and the Purple Heart. My wound is healed (rt. hand) and I'm as healthy as a jack-rabbit. Things are certainly looking fine and I have great hopes of seeing you soon.

My Darling Margy

While I was in Paris, I had my picture made and will send them to you when I receive them. I didn't get to see them so don't know what they will be like (I had on my new jacket).

I've seen some very interesting and beautiful places, have been in the Alps and now I'm ready to see Florida again.

Please write and tell me all about your V-E. day celebrations- what went on and what you thought. Ours was very quiet as it was sort of an anti-climax. We didn't do any hell raising, we just sat quietly, got a bit tight and felt that a great load had been removed. We talked and thought about home, our loved ones and wished that we could be with you. It was a feeling of relief and we took it that way.

Darling, I miss you and now that I'm not busy want you all the more. Give my love to all the family — I hope to see you soon.

I love and adore you with all my heart.

Forever yours,
Frank

〜

June 14, 1945

Drove thru the Brenner Pass today and rejoined the unit at Rina, Italy, on Lake Garda. This is a very beautiful place and it was great seeing the old gang again.

VJ Day August 1945

Dr. Chunn Remembered
Photographs and Reminiscences

Charles Francis Chunn
1912-1970

                    My Darling Margy

Frank Chunn, June 1935, receiving M.D. degree from Duke University School of Medicine, Durham NC.

Marjorie Moore Chunn, August 1944, receiving a B.S. degree from Florida State College for Women (FSCW), Tallahassee FL. By September of that year, men were attending the school and it was renamed Florida State University (FSU).

Official correspondence from The White House.

FDR's "Letter to Soldiers."

Second Auxiliary Surgical Group, Lawson General Hospital, Atlanta, Georgia, December, 1942.

Major Charles Francis Chunn, January 1943. His official military photograph.

My Darling Margy

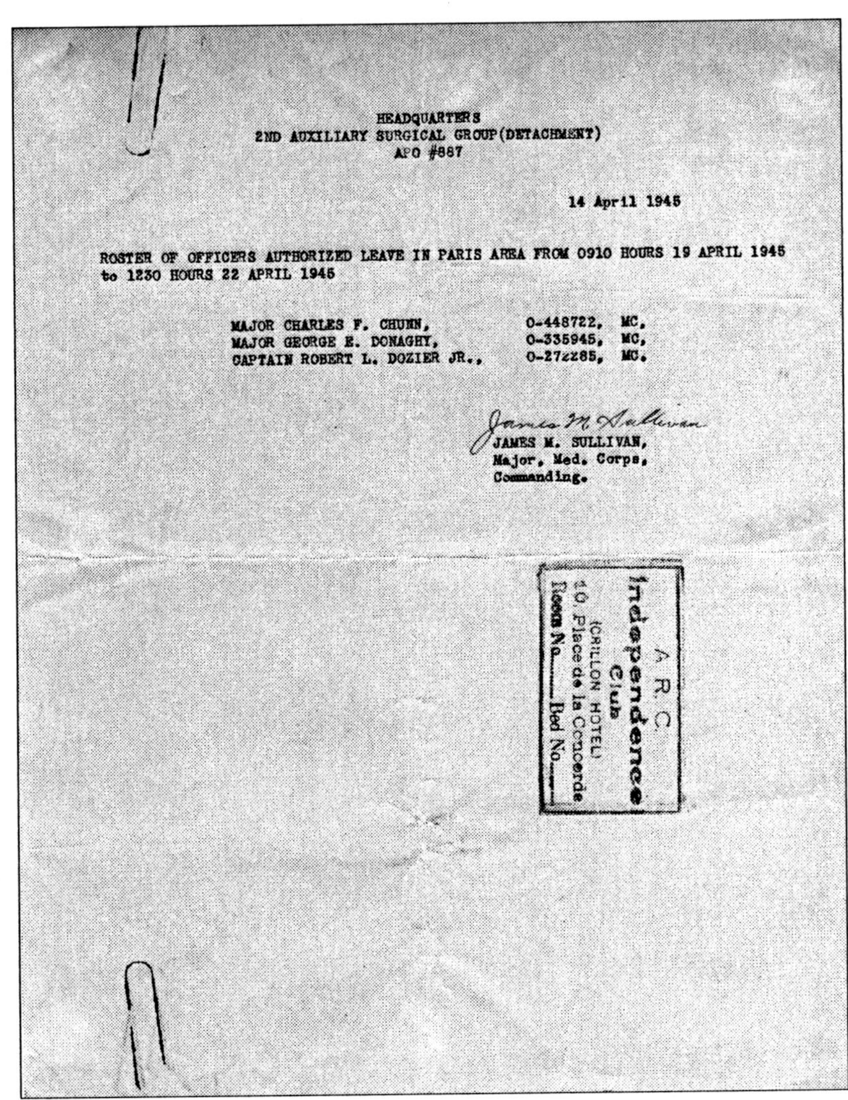

Official Army orders granting Major Chunn a short leave in Paris, April 1943.

Major Chunn enjoying his leave in Paris,
April 1943.

My Darling Margy

HEADQUARTERS
ATLANTIC BASE SECTION
APO 759

4732

25 April 1943

370.5 ABGCT (4-25-43)

Subject: Troop Movement

To   : Commanding Officer
         2nd Auxiliary Surgical Gp.

1. PAC radio Ref. No. 5614, AFHQ, 24 April 1943, the Surgical Teams, 2nd Auxiliary Surgical Group, listed below will proceed without delay from RABAT, French Morocco, by rail and air to destination indicated:

SURGICAL TEAM	DESTINATION
Nos. 18 and 23	Bone, Algeria
Nos. 21 and 22	Phillipeville, Algeria
Nos. 12 and 16	Algiers, Algeria

Officers and nurses will move by air; enlisted men and supplies by rail.

2. Upon arrival at destination, Teams No. 18 and No. 23 will report to the Commanding Officer, 5th General Hospital (BR) for temporary duty, will be relieved from attachment to ABS and will be attached to EBS for supply and administration; Teams No. 21 and No. 22 will report to the Commanding Officer, 67th General Hospital (BR) for temporary duty, will be relieved from attachment to ABS and will be attached to EBS for supply and administration; Team No. 12 will report to the Commanding Officer, 94th General Hospital (BR) for temporary duty, will be relieved from attachment to ABS and will be attached to Hq. Comd., NATOUSA, for supply and administration; Team No. 16 will report to the Commanding Officer, 95th General Hospital (BR) for temporary duty, will be relieved from attachment to ABS and will be attached to Hq. Comd., NATOUSA, for supply and administration.

3. Five (5) days rations will be carried on the rail movement.

4. Surgical instruments and personal equipment will be transported. Such surgical equipment and authorized personal baggage as cannot be transported by air will be transported by rail.

5. The Transportation Corps will furnish the necessary transportation.

- 1 -

Army orders, April 1943, transferring surgical teams from Rabat, French Morocco to duties in Algeria.

Naples,
November
1943.

Germany,
1944.

My Darling Margy

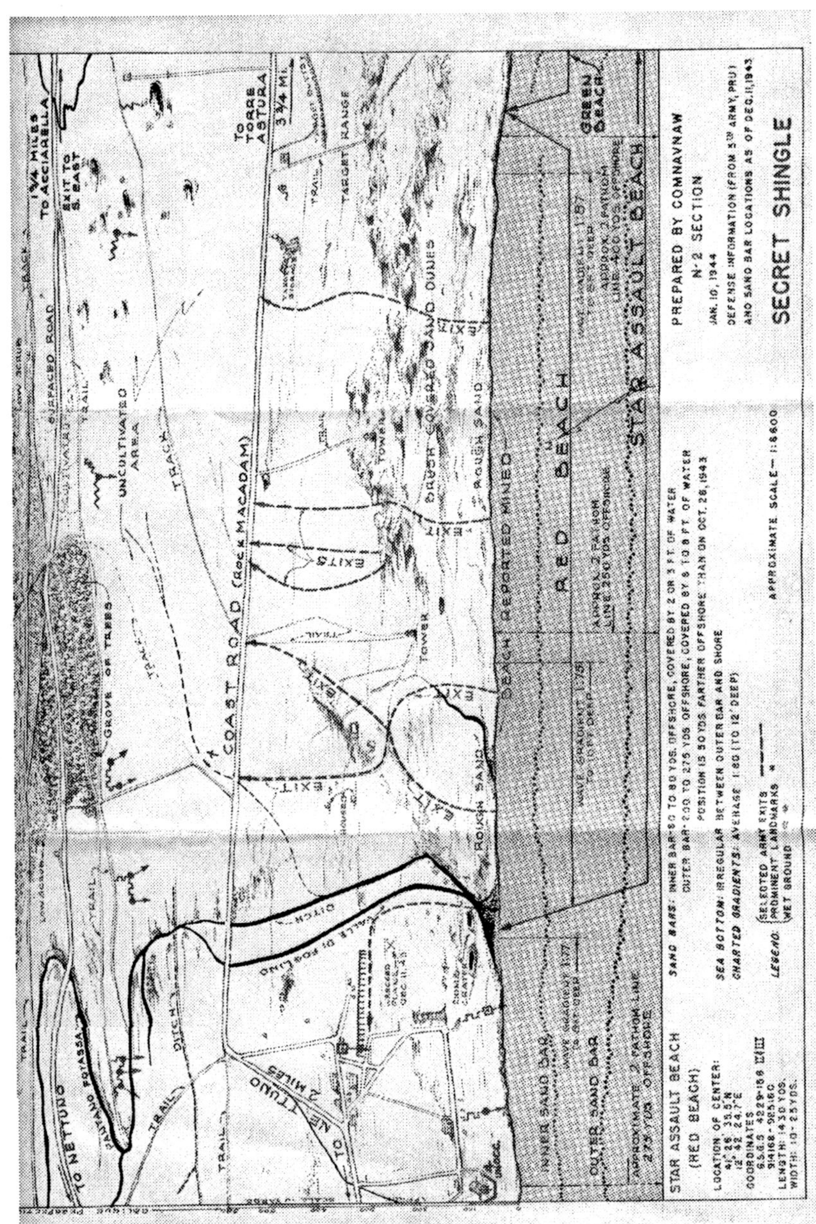

Star Assault Beach, Red Beach portion. Anzio, January 1944. About 35 miles south of Rome, Italy.

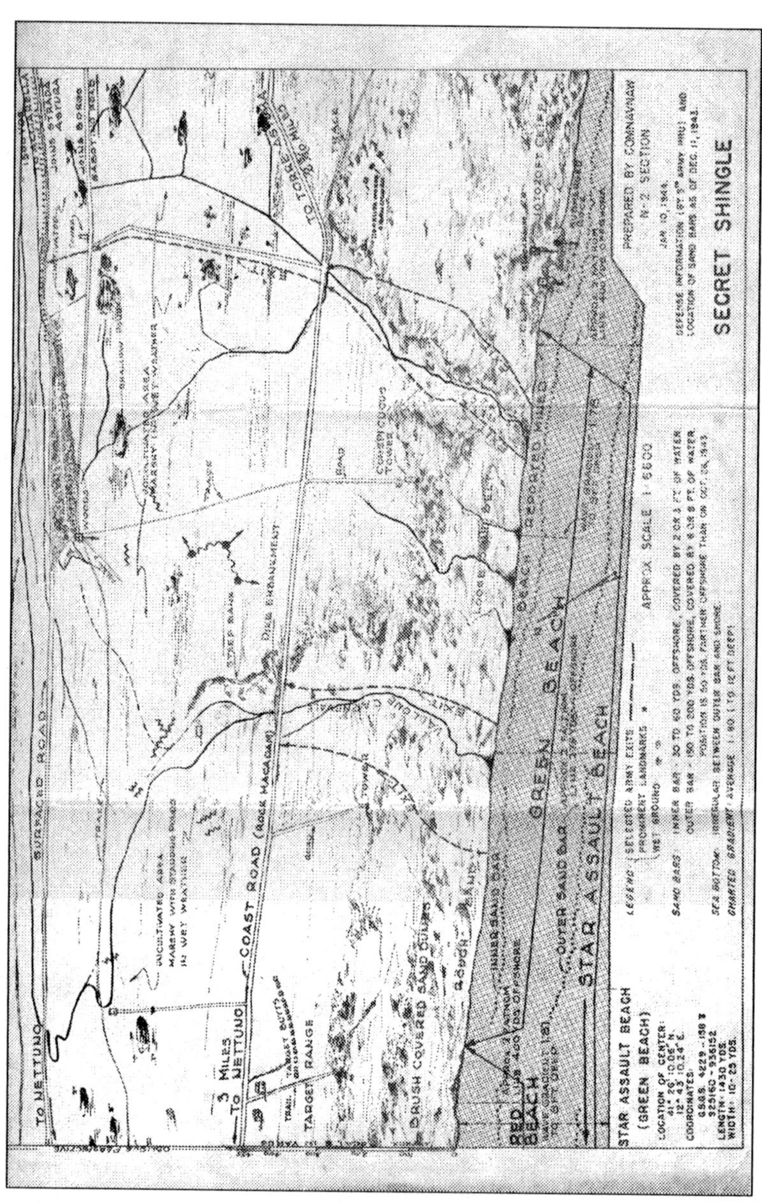

Star Assault Beach, Green Beach portion. Anzio, January 1944. The assault on Anzio resulted in 72,000 casualties in comparison to about 15,000 in the Normandy invasion. (*World War II, America at War 1941-1945,* Norman Polmar & Thomas B. Allen, 1991, Random House, NY)

118   *My Darling Margy*

Paperwork at Anzio, 1944.

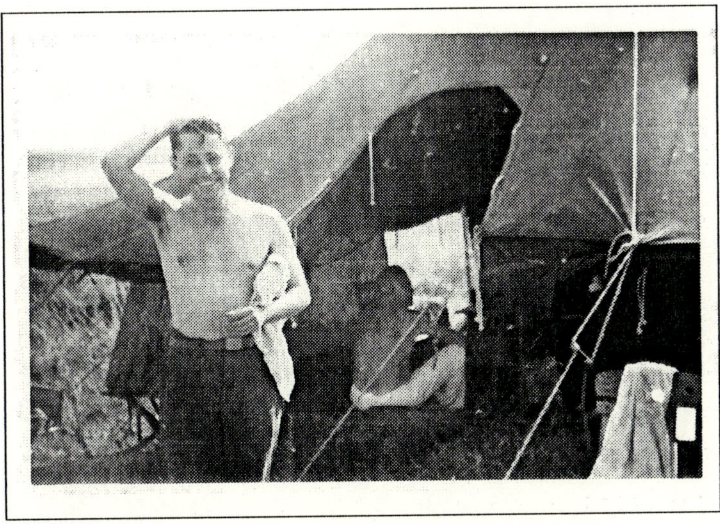

Anzio, Major Chunn bathing from his helmet.

Anzio, 1944.

Anzio, 1944.
Written on back:
Remember when the German artillery shell hit on us while
at the 32nd Field Hosp at Anzio. Lavern F, & Hurt's nurse
— one from the 32nd Field Hosp were both killed instantly.
They were standing out in front of their tent about 5pm when
it hit on top of them.

Visiting the Sistine Chapel, June 1944.

My Darling Margy

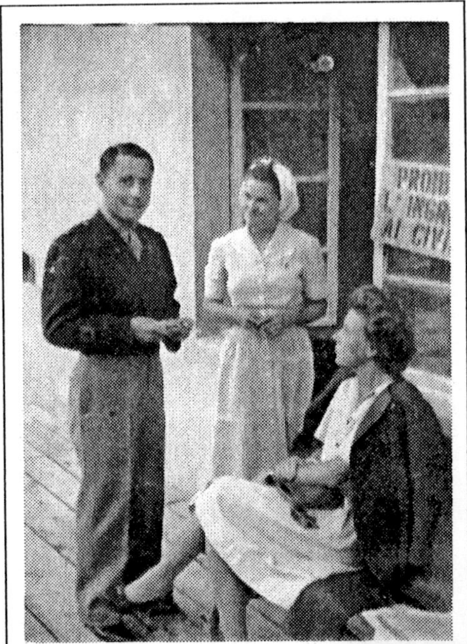

November 1944, France.

France, Major
Chunn on left.

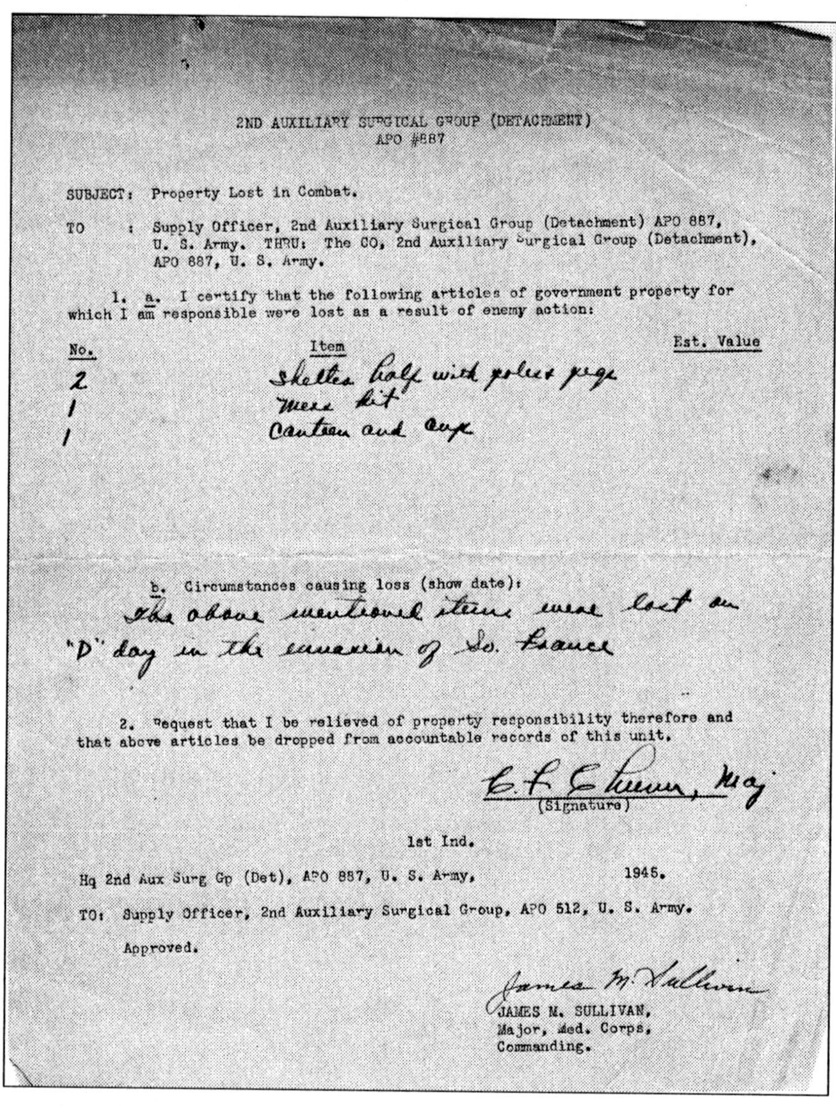

2ND AUXILIARY SURGICAL GROUP (DETACHMENT)
APO #887

SUBJECT: Property Lost in Combat.

TO   : Supply Officer, 2nd Auxiliary Surgical Group (Detachment) APO 887,
          U. S. Army. THRU: The CO, 2nd Auxiliary Surgical Group (Detachment),
          APO 887, U. S. Army.

    1. a. I certify that the following articles of government property for
which I am responsible were lost as a result of enemy action:

No.   Item   Est. Value

2   Shelter half with poles & pegs
1   Mess kit
1   Canteen and cup

        b. Circumstances causing loss (show date):
The above mentioned items were lost on
"D" day in the invasion of So. France

    2. Request that I be relieved of property responsibility therefore and
that above articles be dropped from accountable records of this unit.

                                        E. F. Chunn, Maj.
                                            (Signature)

                                 1st Ind.

Hq 2nd Aux Surg Gp (Det), APO 887, U. S. Army,   1945.

TO: Supply Officer, 2nd Auxiliary Surgical Group, APO 512, U. S. Army.

    Approved.

                                        James M. Sullivan
                                      JAMES M. SULLIVAN,
                                      Major, Med. Corps,
                                      Commanding.

Paperwork documenting U. S. Army property lost by Major
Chunn on "D" Day in Southern France.

                                   My Darling Margy

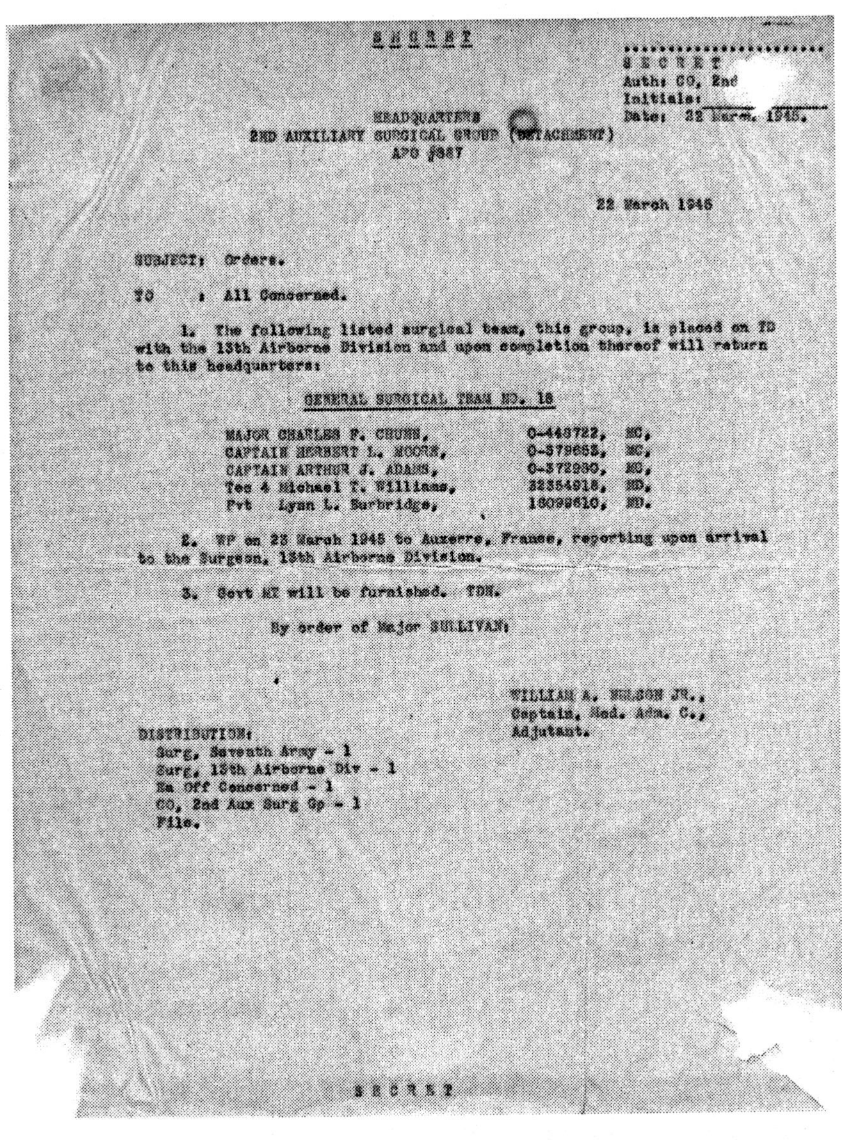

Secret orders temporarily detailing surgical team #18 to the 13th Airborne Division, March 22, 1945. This mission was called off 24 hours later.

THESE SPACES FOR MESSAGE CENTER ONLY

| TIME FILED | MSG CEN No. | HOW SENT |

MESSAGE (SUBMIT TO MESSAGE CENTER IN DUPLICATE) — PRECEDENCE

No. 1 DATE 09 APRIL 1945

To GEN. PIBURN, CCA 10th AD

REQUEST PERMISSION TO EVACUATE WOUNDED BY RETURNING TRANSPORT PLANES AS SOON AS POSSIBLE. TO DATE HAVE 35 PT. ANTICIPATE MORE.

SURGEON 2ND AUX. SURG. GROUP — 2140

OFFICIAL DESIGNATION OF SENDER — TIME SIGNED

B.F. Brown, Maj, MC

SIGNATURE AND GRADE OF WRITER

Urgent message requesting evacuation of wounded from behind enemy lines.

     My Darling Margy

NAME AND ARMY SERIAL NUMBER

O-448722
CHUNN, CHARLES F.

GRADE	COMPANY	REGIMENT AND ARM OR SERVICE
MAJ.	2ND AUX SURG. GR.	—

DIVISION	CORPS	ARMY	AGE	RACE	NATIVITY	SERVICE, YEARS
VI	7TH	32	W	FLA	3

STATION WHERE TAGGED:

CLR. STA 10AD (COA)

DATE 10 APR 45   HOUR 1700

DIAGNOSIS: IF INJURY, STATE HOW, WHEN, WHERE INCURRED

W.I.A. BOMB W. (MORTAR) PEN W. R. HAND AT 1600 ON CRAILSHEIM, GR. AIRFIELD

LINE OF DUTY   YES

TREATMENT:
Dressing
Penicillin

ANTITETANIC SERUM: DOSE   TIME

MORPHINE: DOSE   TIME

DISPOSITION: TRF FIELD HOSP

DATE 10 APR 45   HOUR 1730

SIGNATURE, WITH RANK AND ORGANIZATION:

Form 52b—MEDICAL DEPARTMENT, U. S. A.
(Revised October 25, 1940)
16—15434

Wounded In Action (WIA). Treatment disposition form, details Chunn's injury and disposition. April 1945.

HEADQUARTERS
2ND AUXILIARY SURGICAL GROUP
APO 534 U.S. ARMY

9 June 1944.

SUBJECT: Commendation.

TO   : MAJOR CHARLES F. CHUNN, MC, 2nd Auxiliary
           Surgical Group.

   Since the early organization of this unit you have been the operating surgeon on a general surgical team of this group. Your excellent professional skill, operative technique and surgical judgment have always been outstanding. During the entire period of the Anzio, Italy beachhead operation; you demonstrated these talents under the most difficult and dangerous conditions. Your landing with the assault forces and your sincere desire to remain in this hazardous location in order to make your services available to the wounded soldier, are highly commendable. Your interest and efforts in contributing to the high standards of this organization have merited the highest praise. Your forcefulness and tireless efforts have materially contributed to the development of a most efficient surgical team. The excellent surgical care which you and your team have given the wounded soldier, will be appreciated by many families and many homes throughout the Allied nations long after this war is over.

   I commend you for your outstanding devotion to duty and look forward to continued and even greater achievements.

JAMES H. FORSEE,
Colonel, Med. Corps,
Commanding.

Army commendation for Major Chunn from Commanding Officer, Colonel James Forsee, MD.

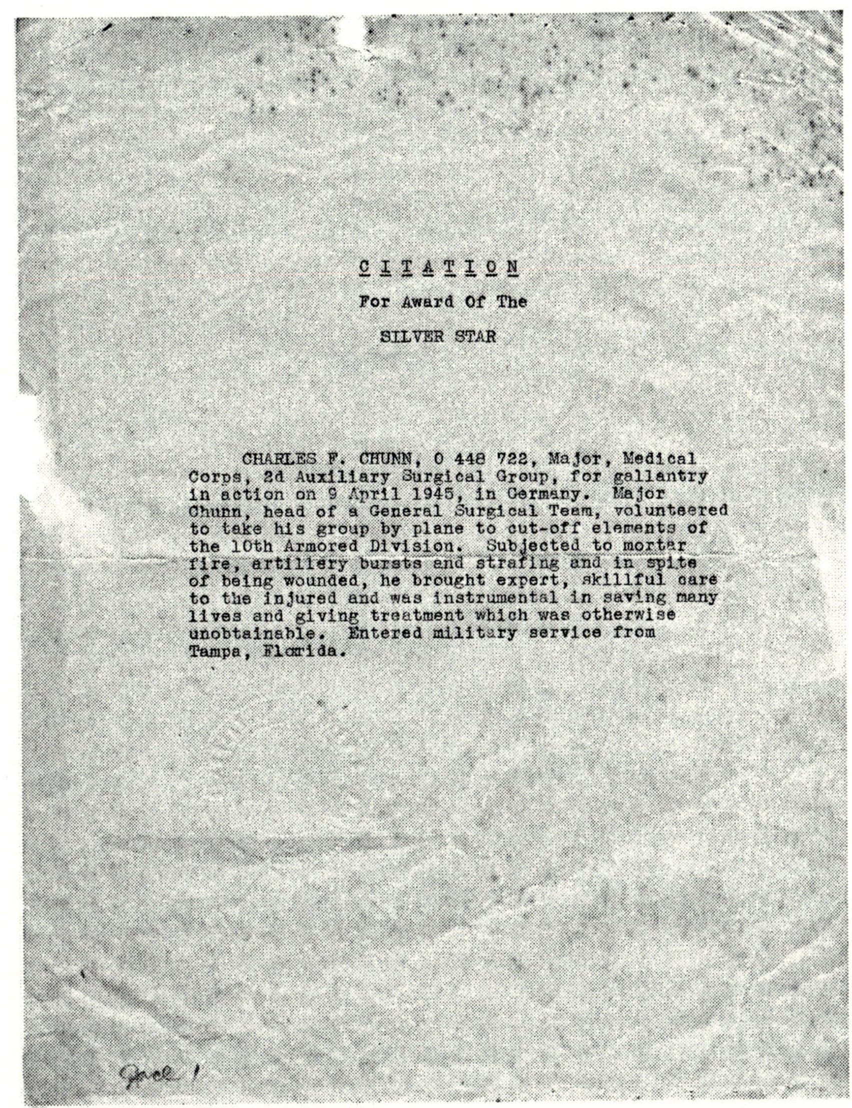

Chunn's award of the Silver Star.
This decoration was established by Act of Congress on July 9, 1918, to recognize heroism in combat. It is awarded only in wartime.

Major Chunn on left. Unknown location.

    My Darling Margy

Anzio, 1944.

Private transportation, unknown location.

Mail to the U.S. from overseas passed through careful scrutiny of the censors.

My Darling Margy

Dr. Chunn's decorations from European Theater, Purple Heart and Silver Star. The Purple Heart decoration was established August 7, 1782, by General George Washington. It is awarded to U.S. personnel for wounds suffered in combat.

Three small bound notebooks — the diaries kept by
Major Frank Chunn. As each book was filled, Chunn
found a method of transporting it back to Margy. A patient
returning to a stateside hospital would hand carry it with
instructions to mail it to her once he was back in America.

My Darling Margy

Frank Chunn collected sterling silver bracelets for Margy during his moves through Africa. Each was engraved with a place — Casablanca, Algiers, Bizerte, Tunis, Rabat, Constantine and Bone. When Chunn left Africa, he entrusted the bracelets to a pilot who was returning to the States. The pilot was able to get them safely to Margy.

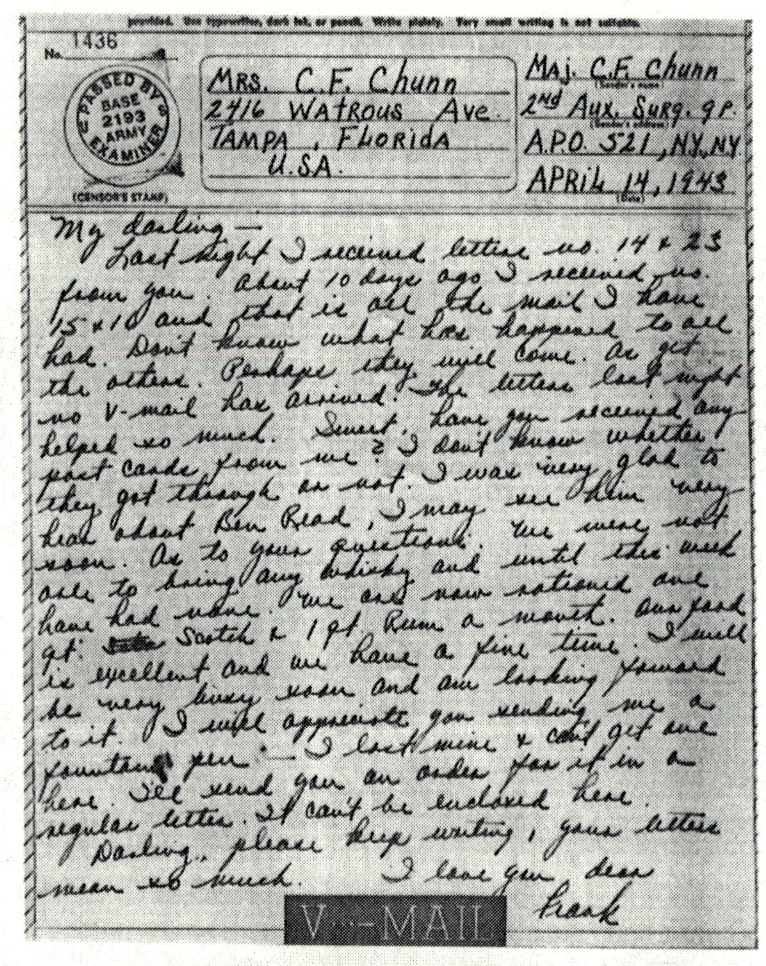

No. 1436
PASSED BY BASE 2193 ARMY EXAMINER
(CENSOR'S STAMP)
Mrs. C.F. Chunn
2416 Watrous Ave.
Tampa, Florida
U.S.A.
Maj. C.F. Chunn
2nd Aux. Surg. Gp.
A.P.O. 521, N.Y, N.Y
April 14, 1943
My darling —
Last night I received letters no. 14 & 23
from you. About 10 days ago I received no.
15 & 18 and that is all the mail I have
had. Don't know what has happened to all
the others. Perhaps they will come. As yet
no v-mail has arrived. The letters last night
helped so much. Sweet, have you received any
post cards from me? I don't know whether
they got through or not. I was very glad to
hear about Ben Read. I may see him very
soon. As to your questions: we were not
able to doing any drinking and until this week
have had none. We are now rationed one
qt. Scotch & 1 pt. Rum a month. Our food
is excellent and we have a fine time. I will
be very busy soon and am looking forward
to it. I will appreciate you sending me a
fountain pen — I lost mine & can't get one
here. I'll send you an order for it in a
regular letter. It can't be enclosed here.
Darling, please keep writing, your letters
mean so much. I love you dear
Frank
V · MAIL

"Condensed letters were sent to and from U.S.
servicemen and servicewomen overseas. After being
written and posted, the letters were photographed on
microfilm. Then the rolls were transported to distribution
centers where they were enlarged to four-by-five inch
prints and put into conventional postal delivery systems.
'Write plainly,' the correspondents were warned on
the V-Mail form. 'Very small writing is not suitable.'
About 150 words fit on the form. The logo for this mail,
encompassing the Morse code for V, was V...– Mail."

—From *World War II, America at War 1941-1945*, Norman
Polmar and Thomas B. Allen, Random House, 1991.

Post Script

Celeste Chunn Colcord

The third diary ends abruptly with the August 1945 announcement of VJ Day— victory for the U.S. in Japan. Nothing more about clean-up operations or the massive process of returning thousands of anxious soldiers to the United States from Europe. Frank Chunn was tired and he had noted that VE Day was anticlimactic. His love of adventure would return, but at this point it had been worn down by the seemingly endless realities of war and death.

Many people have read these diaries over the past sixty years. Friends that knew Frank Chunn and how he lived after the war, simply read and understood more about the man. Others that didn't know him, asked questions about what happened next. Those reading with a critical eye noted that there was no ending to the story.

So we asked my mother to respond and fill in the details for an ending. She has done so and what follows is the story of a man's life after a war experience. She doesn't tell you he was a charismatic leader or a benevolent tyrant in the surgical suite, but she tells of his love for family, for healing and for fun.

My brother and sister wanted to write an epilogue and their voices are here too. We were all affected by the dynamo personality that fathered us. Ethel Howard writes from the dimension of meeting Dr. Chunn as a seriously ill patient. My cousins, Mike and Carol, wanted to examine the influence their uncle had on their lives and tell their stories. In a remarkable coincidence, one of my father's chief surgical enemies of wartime, shock, was addressed years later by Mike's pioneering invention for blood pressure monitoring.

Epilogue
Marjorie Chunn Cochran

The Second Aux had to stay on in Italy for three months after the war ended in Europe. They recreated on Lake Garda in north Italy while writing up their cases and reports. The Second Aux was known for performing the most battle surgery in World War II, and their records showed that Major Chunn had done more than any other surgeon. *Forward Surgery of the Severely Wounded, by the Second Auxiliary Surgical Group, 1942-1945* is the book published from the reports written in Garda after the war ended. The second section, "Wounds of the Colon and Rectum," was authored by Major Chunn and his colleague, Major Richard V. Hauver.

When the book was ready to be published, the guys agreed it was time to go home. Frank had once volunteered to go to the Pacific Theater, but the war was over there, too, and Frank went to Naples and boarded a liberty ship headed to the U.S. It took thirteen days and then several days on a troop train to Camp Blanding at Starke, Florida, where he was "separated" from the army. I met him in Starke and we had a short vacation. He was promoted to lieutenant colonel but did not stay in the Army Reserve. He was later a consultant for MacDill Air Force Base, Tampa, and Bay Pines Veterans Hospital nearby.

We bought our first home in South Tampa and started a private surgical practice at 442 W. Lafayette Street, where many of the returning doctors reopened after their absence. The practice boomed and there were hospital staffs and social organizations to join. Later we were asked to join in founding Palma Ceia United Methodist Church. Frank had a nurse and a secretary working for him. I was busy trying to follow Dr. Parsons' admonition, "A wife can be a doctor's most valuable asset." Soon we were expecting our first child. We had Clorinda, named for Grandmother Chunn, and she would be called "Cloe." She was adorable and such a joy to everyone. Frank would always awaken her to play and spoil her.

In less than two years we had Charles Francis Chunn, Jr., "Frankie," who was just as remarkable and loved as much as his sister. They were dressed alike sometimes, and looked like twins. Frank would take them to see his patients on Sunday mornings. Soon we had outgrown our little house on Bay Villa, and we found a house that suited us on the fifth fairway of Palma Ceia Golf Course. Of course we kept doing things to the house as our needs changed, like building a carport (the garage was filled with washer, dryer, and kids' playthings.) The back yard had a wading pool, swings, and a whirligig. The pebble driveway had to be concreted for skates, tricycles, and parties. We always had parties for the kids' birthdays, and took movies with the little camera we brought from Detroit.

Besides the children's parties, our house was open to parties for the garden club, cancer society, new interns, and Hillsborough County Medical Auxiliary. Frank would call me to keep overnight a patient who missed a train or flight. We were a celebrating bunch of aunts, uncles, cousins, grandparents, and grandchildren. All birthdays were celebrated, with the Christmas, Easter, and Thanksgiving holidays rotating among our four extended family households.

When Cloe was born, Ethel Howard came as an angel to our family. After a very critical illness she started taking care of our new baby girl. Ethel had moved to Tampa from Lesley, Georgia, where she had a fifth grade education. She was interested in learning about everything, and diligently studied the Bible. She

   My Darling Margy

was so loving and kind, we all depended on her for her spiritual love. She has had many disappointments but has remained one of our best loved friends. Although she has endeared herself to many others, we are proud that she is still known as Ethel Chunn.

Frank was such a dedicated doctor—he never failed to put patients first. He missed Frankie's Christening and his graduation from McCallie Prep School. He belonged to several surgical organizations and took time for those, but seldom took vacations. He hated not to see his post-operative patients himself every day. He made house calls, which is what he was doing three hours before he himself died.

Frank had hobbies that would absorb him. At our country home on Keystone Lake, he labored hard enclosing ten acres, digging post holes and stringing barbed wire, in order to keep a few white faced Hereford cattle. He cared for them, even delivering a calf when the vet couldn't come. Of course, I was there to assist (as I did when he cut and shaped our Doberman pinscher's ears). He spent hours running our little motor boat pulling the children on water skis. Our lake house was sometimes used by the convent of nuns who administrated and worked in St. Joseph's Hospital, where Frank worked side by side with them daily. The nuns spent time on retreat at the lake, and at times Frank would also be present. He taught some of them to drive the tractor. He was an enthusiastic and energetic hobby farmer, experimented with welding, and learned to use various tools to restore an old Jeep. He also was fond of new cars, and tried out a Thunderbird, various Cadillacs, and a short-lived Toronado.

Frank introduced Frankie to hunting, and they spent time hunting on a ranch near Arcadia. They went on fishing trips from Clearwater Beach for several summers and sometimes at Boca Grande.

When Cloe was eight and Frankie was six, the greatest thing
to happen to our family was the coming of Celeste Moore
Chunn, our new baby girl. She was the toy of the children, and
everybody's little angel. She was always with us and held her
own with dignity and love. We added a nursery and enlarged
the family room, and built a hospitable patio with a Mexican
fire pit we used frequently for lobster and clam bakes. A grateful
and endearing patient of Frank's shipped us lobster from Maine
and brought us birch logs for our fireplace. This dear lady died
and willed Frank her elegant possessions from two homes. We
shared furniture, china, lamps, and heirlooms with relatives and
friends—our family has always referred to her as "Aunt Dorothy."

Cloe went off for four years and graduated from Duke University.
Frankie spent two years at Tulane University and then transferred
to the University of Florida (from which he graduated after his
father's death). Celeste was at Berkeley Prep in Tampa.

Frank worked steadily and took time to go fishing on his boat in
Tampa Bay. He would take groups of two or three doctors and
sometimes nurses or friends. Many times just he and I would go.
In June 1969 our family took a ten day cruise on this boat named
Celeste stopping over at Boca Grande, Useppa, and Captiva
islands— it was wonderful our all being together.

Frank had served on several boards of surgical societies, had been
President of the Hillsborough County Medical Society and for
many years on the Board of Governors of the American College
of Surgeons. When it met annually, the 2nd Aux would have its
annual reunion. This was when they re-lived their World War
II experiences and they rejoiced seeing each other and mourned
those unable to return. The last reunion he attended was October
1969. Several members had visited us in Tampa over the years.

                                    My Darling Margy

After Christmas, Cloe became engaged to Larry Catlett, a Tampa medical student at Emory University. They were to marry in June 1970. Our lives were all extra busy and we were planning the wedding and had the invitations ready to be addressed.

Frank and I were at the Tampa Yacht Club aboard the *Celeste*, buttoning her up so we could attend a meeting in Detroit. All of a sudden, his color changed and he began gasping. I screamed for helped and an ambulance and started CPR – the help came, and much later, the ambulance. It was his last ride to St. Joseph Hospital. The diagnosis was "myocardial infarction."

That April 16, 1970, he had done an operation, made a house call on Davis Island and had gone to a doctor's office for an EKG. When he came home for lunch, he told me that he had been having pains in his left arm for several days. The EKG had looked normal so he ate a little lunch, changed clothes and asked me to drive him to get the boat ready for our absence.

It was the last day of an extraordinary life. A life that gave life and improved life for so many.

Cloe's Story

Cloe Chunn

I was born Clorinda D'Aubert Chunn in 1947. As the first child and Baby Boomer, I have a longer memory than my brother and sister of our father, who died when I was 22.

Daddy's personal attributes were always energetic—his daily enthusiasm to get up and go to work, his playfulness and exuberance, and his hot temper. He was a man who expressed his emotions truthfully and well. I remember him "rough-housing" with my brother Frankie and me. We fought hard, laughing, happily tearing the household asunder. I remember times when I was afraid of his point blank anger. And times he challenged me to stick to a hard job. And the night my sister Celeste amazed us all with her stunning performance in the Tampa Civic Ballet. We sat enthralled as she floated across the stage without touching it, gliding gracefully like a sacred shimmering dove. I looked at Daddy next to me, and saw the silent tears roll down his face.

Daddy took care of all our family, relatives, and most of the neighborhood. Although our family usually went fishing on Saturdays and ate fish and grits on Saturday night, on Sundays we could often be found at home puttering about the house and yard. The phone would ring, and Daddy would invite the Watsons or whoever it was to come over and "we'll take a look." Sometimes it was a throat, or an ear or tummy, but when someone needed stitches, the whole family went into action. Mama opened the locked closet and got out the sterile instruments she kept ready. We kids cleared off the kitchen table. My job was to hold the spotlight on the minor surgery. Many of our pals sported stitches from our kitchen. One night a drunk teenaged boy passed out in our hedge. Daddy carried him in, checked his vital signs, and put him to bed in our guest room. The next morning, Daddy found out who he was and drove him home.

So I knew I could call on Daddy any time, any time at all. And I sure did. When I was a camp counselor about thirty miles out of Tampa, one of my campers got sick. I called Daddy, and he came right out. A few days later, another boy fell out of a tree and broke his arm. Daddy came as soon as I called, made him comfortable, and drove him home. So, of course, when I became a teacher at Leto High School in Tampa, I knew the number to call the day I took my students to Falk Theater to see *Death of a Salesman*. As we were getting off the bus, one girl twisted her ankle on the bus steps and fell out onto the sidewalk. Another was being helped down by friends who told me she had overdosed. Daddy to the rescue again.

Daddy's rescue services extended to some shenanigans I pulled now and then, too lengthy to describe; suffice it to say I was able to experience both his ever ready rescue service and his appropriate, well-expressed anger.

The greatest of rescue stories was told to me long after it happened by Ethel Howard, our dear family friend and employee, to whom my brother, sister, and I refer as our "Other Mother." Ethel came to Tampa from Georgia, after leaving the farm of her birthplace with her husband Lee. In her early twenties, new in town, Ethel became very ill, so ill with intestinal obstructions that she was nearly dead when Daddy was called. He did long hours of surgery on Ethel, and he knew she needed undivided attention for the first 24 hours after surgery. In those days Tampa had two hospitals, one for whites and one for blacks. Daddy took call and worked at both hospitals, and he did Ethel's surgery at Tampa Negro Hospital. Afterward, he ordered a private duty nurse for the first 24 hours in Ethel's room. The nursing staff told him they were too short handed to provide the service. Daddy asked, "Then do you have a cot you can set up in her room?" Daddy stayed in Ethel's room for 24 hours to see her safely through. At the end of this story Ethel smiled softly and said, "And, Cloe, it was his birthday."

When Ethel recovered, Daddy liked her so much he offered her a job because Mama was about to give birth to me. Ethel began working for our family then, and became one of my most important mentors. She still works one day a week for Mama, 58 years later, mostly so they can see each other. Ethel and Daddy had a special fondness for each other, and to this day, Ethel never turns a stray cat away from her door. "It just might be Dr. Chunn," she says with an expectant sparkle.

And that is the best way I can describe who Daddy was. He had his shortcomings, his prejudices about race, politics, various "isms" and groups. But at the individual level, when Daddy could help someone, no matter who it was, he knocked himself out to help. And purely for the joy of helping. My greatest learning from him is that when something is right to do, you don't wait to be told, and you don't expect anything in return. We do it because it is the right thing to do, and we do it with all our might.

Frank's Story

C. Frank Chunn (Jr.)

I have been most fortunate to have had an interesting, enjoyable and fruitful life as my father's namesake, Charles Francis "Frank" Chunn Jr. This has been the direct result of my father's guidance and influence during the first twenty years of my life until his death at the young age of 56. Dad taught me many of life's values and morals which can best be summed up with the words of his, and my, most favorite poem *If* by Rudyard Kipling. I still have the old antique copy of that poem that he gave to me framed on the wall of my office.

Not only did he teach life's values and ethics but he taught compassion for his fellow man. I have never met a more compassionate person than my father. His compassion extended to everyone he touched: his family, his friends, his medical associates and his patients….and, oh, how his patients loved and adored him. Throughout my life and even today, 35 years after his death, I encounter people in Tampa who say to me, "Frank Chunn? Are you related to the Dr. Chunn?" Then, with a proud and affirmative reply of "Yes, he was my father," I always get a wonderful story of a life saving surgery, a caring "bedside manner" and utmost admiration and gratitude for his medical attention.

In remembering stories about grateful patients I will never forget one that comes to mind with little bit of a different twist to it. When I was 15 years old two of my best buddies and I were bass fishing in our secret pond back in the woods in north Tampa. The local game warden came walking through the woods, approached us and asked to see our fishing licenses. Not being able to produce fishing licenses, the game warden proceeded

to take our names and address. When I replied, he asked, "are
you Dr. Frank Chunn's son?" Thinking this was our ticket
to freedom, I quickly replied "Yes Sir, Officer". The reply was
this, "well your Daddy just got through reaming me a new rear
end and I didn't appreciate it a bit. He told me the best thing
for the dadgum pain was to sit in a hot bath tub with a bottle
of whiskey." After about 30 minutes in his patrol car, and us
thinking we were all going to jail, with a twinkle in his eye and a
smirk on his face he said, " get outta' here and don't let me catch
y'all again without a fishing license. Later I learned that the game
warden had had a successful, but painful, hemorrhoid operation
performed by Dr. Chunn.

Christmas was always special at our house because of the many,
many wonderful gifts delivered during the holidays by Dad's
grateful and adoring patients. I think surgical bills were paid
in some cases with bushels of oranges and outstanding Cuban
delicacies.

Not only did Dad teach valuable lessons in life but he taught
me many things that I continue to love in my life. We shared a
passion for outdoor sports during our time together. He taught
me about gun safety, shooting and hunting, and fishing and
boating and many other things too.

I can remember as a very little boy going with him to the marina
where he kept his boat. While he worked on the boat, he would
keep me entertained with a cane pole and shrimp fishing off the
back of the boat. One afternoon I surprised us all with a fine
catch of redfish and snapper of which a photograph made the
Tampa Tribune sports page a week later. Dad was very proud of
his "chip off the ole block," Splinter, which was my nickname at
the time. He kept that photograph of me and the stringer of fish
on his office wall the rest of his life.

                                    My Darling Margy

Several wonderful summer vacations were spent with the family cruising down to southwest Florida, fishing and sightseeing along the way, on his 37 foot Chris Craft motor yacht named after my sister, Celeste. Other summers were spent at Clearwater Beach were we would fish days and crab nights with family and friends. One of my fondest recollections about my Mom and Dad occurred during one night of crabbing on the beach. The men and kids loaded up on blue crabs, catching them with nets and lanterns while wading in the surf. Washtub after washtub full of live blue crabs were delivered to Mom for boiling and cleaning who promptly carried them over to the bay in back of the house and dumped them over the seawall to freedom. I'm not sure Dad ever knew the better.

Dad and I shared a passion for firearms and he amassed a fine collection of all types but mainly muzzle loading Kentucky rifles. We participated together in several "beef shoots" (competitive rifle matches) during summer vacations at the Cataloochee Ranch in Maggie Valley, North Carolina, where Dad was fondly dubbed the "Singin' Cowboy" by the ranch hands for his flamboyant cowboy shirts, boots and Stetson hats.

We once went on a muzzleloader rifle buying jaunt into the backwoods mountains near Waynesville, North Carolina, in search of a particular local rifle maker. We found the rifle maker, purchased a rifle and during the friendship that ensued Dad diagnosed his new friend with a serious form of cancer. He then quickly proceeded to arrange treatment for him in a local hospital. I don't know whatever happened to Mr. Farmer but I'm sure his life was prolonged by Dr. Chunn's swift medical attention. Subsequently, in a photograph which appeared in the *Tampa Tribune* article about my Dad and me with our rifles, I am holding that same J. W. Farmer made Kentucky rifle which is a cherished part of my collection today.

Another one of Dad's hobbies worth mentioning was gentleman farming. For a number of years, we owned a lake place just outside of Tampa called Chunn's Cove (after the well known North Carolina mountaineer clan's homestead) on 22 acres of land, complete with boats, a barn, a tractor with numerous farm implements and a bright red 1947 Ford pickup truck in which Dad was frequently seen driving the country roads. We had horses and cows in the pasture but I'll never forget the day when Dr. Chunn's recent purchase of two pure bred black angus steers were delivered. He was ever so proud of those animals. Later that day he and I went out to check on them…. I can picture him now walking around the corner of the barn. Well, the next thing I see – here he comes, back around the corner of the barn, full speed, with the two steers in close pursuit! I had never seen my Dad run before but let me tell you he was fast. I guess he never quite made peace with those critters because several months after that incident we were enjoying fine farm raised black angus steaks.

My sister, Cloe, has referred to Dad's temper in her narrative so I feel compelled to comment on that. I guess he did have a bit of a temper and I think that I honestly inherited mine from him. Though I really only saw it a few times , one incident that Mom and I still laugh about to this day was the time I refused his offer of a free haircut.

One summer, it seems as though I let my hair grow a little longer than to his liking. He handed me $10 and told me to get a trim. After refusing his offer, I went to my room and locked the door. Big mistake. Moments later here comes dad with the axe, past Mom, ready to splinter the door. Mom quickly interceded, defused the situation and I went and got a haircut.

I have never seen a man more loved and admired by his friends and colleagues than Dad. He was totally dedicated to his patients

                                    My Darling Margy

and his love of healing and surgery and though he spent most of
his waking life in the hospital operating room or with patients,
he still made time for family and friends. His love of life and
everything it presented was contagious to everyone around him.
As you have gathered from his diaries his spare time was filled
with fun, adventure, friendship and the finer enjoyments in life.
He was always up for a good party and could come up with a
good reason to celebrate most any occasion he and his friends
contrived. It never interfered with his medical practice or patient
care.

For as long as I can remember Dad worked in private practice
seven days a week. He was first on the operating room schedule
Monday through Friday with patient rounds after surgery
and office hours in the afternoons. Hospital rounds to check
on patients were made every Saturday and Sunday morning.
Thursday, Saturday and Sunday afternoons were Dad's "R & R"
time. He could usually be found "puttering" on his boat or at
Chunn's Cove or fishing in the bay or tinkering with his guns
— never far away from the telephone where he could be reached
by the hospital in the event of an emergency. Late night phone
calls and house calls were the norm for him. I still have the black
leather "doctor's bag" he had on ready in the trunk of his car (I
bet they don't even make those kinds of bags anymore).

At one point in my adolescence, I thought that I really wanted to
follow in my father's footsteps and become a surgeon. Over time
and after witnessing his absolute dedication to his profession, I
decided that his shoes were just too big to fill. I do not regret that
decision. I just don't think there could ever have been another Dr.
Chunn.

Dad died of a massive heart attack on a Thursday afternoon
in April of 1970 on his boat docked at the Tampa Yacht and

Country Club. Despite the valiant resuscitation efforts by his fellow boaters, dockmaster and the EMS, he could not be saved. The citizens of the City of Tampa, which was still a relatively small close-knit community at the time, poured out their hearts to us and mourned his passing. Though we have many fine physicians and surgeons in our community, Dr. Chunn's legacy has never and will never be forgotten.

Carol's Story
Carol Ramsey Turpin, Niece

Uncle Dockie, as we affectionately called him, was our family's "in house" medical resource for as long as he lived. We knew him first as our doctor-uncle who removed our warts and stitched up our cuts. Later, we would learn he was a skilled battlefield surgeon, a shrewd diagnostician, and the saver of many lives...including my mother's.

It was the middle of December in 1964, the week before my wedding, a stressful time under normal circumstances. My usually healthy mother became ill, and was hospitalized for pneumonia, but Dockie was not so sure. He constantly bird-dogged the hospital testing procedures. Then he and a medical colleague, who had heard one other heart beating with the same peculiar sound and rhythm, made a frightening tentative diagnosis: a ruptured heart.

At that time there were only two heart surgeons in the country qualified to operate on this rare condition. One was Dr. Denton Cooley at St. Luke's Hospital in Houston, Texas. Dockie got on the phone, made a plea for emergency intervention, and was given the go-ahead by Dr. Cooley only if the patient could be brought to Houston for the surgery. Frantically, Dockie called every commercial airline, only to be told that all passengers must be able to sit up for the entire flight; Mother could not. He then called MacDill Air Force Base hoping they had a transport that was pressurized and could make a mercy trip to Houston; they did not. How were they going to save his sister-in-law, Sadie, if he could not get her to Houston? In desperation, he called Jim Walter, a Tampa corporate giant, who graciously offered his private plane and pilot as soon as they could get it ready for a stretcher to board.

That afternoon on the tarmac was a tearful time. Dockie met the ambulance bringing Mother; my Dad and my Aunt Boo (Dockie's wife) and I gathered around to see them off. I cried as mother said to me, trying to make her weak voice stronger, "Now you be a pretty bride." Dockie reassured us he would be with her all the way, as was my Dad, who returned immediately after her surgery in time to walk me down the aisle. Their flight was met by a waiting ambulance that took them to St. Luke's. The ruptured heart diagnosis was confirmed; the open-heart surgery was done while Dockie watched Dr. Cooley's every move. Aunt Boo was an able stand-in for the missing mother of the bride. The prayers of friends were felt as I walked with Dad down the aisle. My new husband and I flew to Houston before going on our honeymoon; Dad was not far behind us. We would all return home on the same day…a joyful reunion at Dockie's house where Mother would convalesce under nurse Aunt Boo's care. Mama's life had been spared, and she lived to see great grandchildren.

Our family was again to be very thankful for Dockie's input and influence. My brother Mike's decision to go into medicine was a result of personal inspiration and practical mentoring from his admired uncle. Not only did Mike follow in his footsteps by going to Duke medical school, but Dockie arranged for Mike's housing in Durham at the home of a fellow doctor and friend who was Dean of the Med School and would soon become the University President. Though Dockie would not live to see the fruition of his nephew's outstanding career in bio-medical engineering, the legacy of a doctor-uncle's advice and encouragement lives on in a doctor-inventor with the same determination for the best of medical care.

Uncle Dockie, indeed, cast a long shadow of medical excellence and patriotic heroism so characteristic of "the greatest generation." For his presence in our lives I shall always be grateful.

My Darling Margy

Ethel's Story
Ethel Howard

Late Saturday afternoon, late May nineteen hundred forty-seven, after two doctors had given up after trying, Dr. Chunn was called. He came in and examined me, called an ambulance and sent me right to Clara Frye Hospital. There he worked pumping my stomach inserting tubes, needles until he was wet with sweat. Diagnosis was intestinal obstruction— the worst case.

Three days later I was told I need to have surgery. That night I needed a nurse, I could not afford one. That night Dr, Chunn stay by my bed side all night. Assured I get the care I needed. I knew the Lord sent him.

So I pray that I be able to work again so I could pay him. Every day he would visit and check how I was. So I ask him if I be able to work again, he assured I would. God works in mysterious ways. He asked me what kind of work I did. At the time I didn't have a regular job. I was doing days for different families. Dr. Chunn ask me if I like to work for him. He explain they were expecting their first baby and he like for me to take care of it. Before the baby came I had surgery again. After recovering I met his lovely wife and baby girl.

[He told Ethel he wanted to "come back as a city cat." She has adopted stray cats at her door and has faithfully tended them and the Chunn family for 58 years. — M. Chunn Cochran]

Memories of My Uncle: Charles Frank Chunn, MD

… and forever Uncle Dockie to me.

Maynard (Mike) Ramsey III, MD, PhD

Writing this is a joy, and the writing process brings back some great memories that I had not replayed in my mind for many years, though much of it is a daily reflection. But this process is painful too, knowing the man, his importance to me, and loving him for 27 years. Where do I start … and how can I end …

Battle Surgeon:
I read his war diary. It's beautiful, and it captures in his own words, his own style, and in his own vivid descriptions the heroic actions of the man I knew, the man I loved as my Uncle Dockie. I've seen his Silver Star and his Purple Heart, they hang framed near a beautiful portrait of him, in his son's home. I've read the commendation for his Silver Star, but it's very much understated, based on what I know. He was one hell of a soldier surgeon. I am so very proud of him, and so thankful that he was my uncle. He changed my life so very much for the better, in many ways, and many times.

His war experiences were all finished, long over actually, before I even knew him. He was at war in North Africa and Europe when I was born in Birmingham, Alabama, where my dad was stationed in the Army Air Force, fighting that same war. My uncle didn't talk much about the war, but as an aspiring surgeon myself, I would ask him to tell me how it was during the war for him as a forward mobile hospital battle surgeon and he told me a few … well, war stories.

To set the stage, he described for me how he and his surgical team were one of the first of a new type of forward-based battlefield surgical hospital. These hospitals were tents, so they were very mobile, and could therefore be positioned close behind the battle lines. They were designed to save our wounded men by providing early surgical treatment or stabilization of their wounds prior to evacuation and they also bolstered the morale of our soldiers by their knowing that surgical medical care was only a short distance from the point of their potential wounding. This type of mobile, forward-placed surgical hospital was later known as a Mobile Army Surgical Hospital (MASH) in the Korean War and inspired the TV series *M*A*S*H*, but this was 10 years earlier in WW II. These mobile surgical hospitals were so close to the enemy lines that Dockie always operated with a Colt .45 automatic pistol on his hip, under his surgical gown. Though they were never overrun by Germans, he said it was close several times, and many times they would continue to operate with incoming mortar and artillery fire.

At the time of my asking him about being a battle surgeon, I had no idea what he had been through in the war, and he told me a small bit of it, but it would be many years later and unfortunately, many years after his death, before his war diaries and letters would be transcribed, and I could read for myself all the vivid, often inspiringly heroic details of his war years. Uncle Dockie had a great sense of humor, and even in his diaries, there are elements of humor, and fun. It was after all, the largest adventure, for better and worse, one could ever live, and though he always put duty first, seeing humor and having fun were an important part of the man too. It was part of what we all loved about him.

He told me some about the war in North Africa, and in Sicily, and about his last theater in World War II, Germany. It is almost 40 years ago, but I vividly remember his recounting some

                                    My Darling Margy

details about a particularly important mission while he was in the German theater. He told me about volunteering to be flown deep into Germany, way behind the enemy lines, because Patton and his tanks had substantially outrun his infantry and was now cutoff, far behind those enemy lines, without supplies and with many wounded soldiers needing treatment. Uncle Dockie's mission was to fly in, with his surgical team and minimal surgical gear, set up shop in a tavern turned hospital, and operate on many wounded soldiers from Patton's army. Limb wounds, abdominal wounds, chest wounds … my uncle, then the consummate battlefield surgeon by all accounts, could and did, do it all. Later, when I was with him in the O.R., to watch him operate was like watching a poet and an athlete and a watch maker fused into one, focused on a lifesaving task that needed them all at their best, and he always delivered. He was my inspiration to become a surgeon, and he was always my physician-surgeon role model. He remains the most skillful surgeon I have ever assisted, or watched operate, in my life.

On this particular mission into enemy territory in Germany (his Silver Star and Purple Heart were for this one), Uncle Dockie was hit in his right hand by a mortar fragment shortly after landing behind enemy lines. All of the following 36 hours of continuous surgery on our wounded were done with a mortar fragment in his dominant hand. I'm humbled and inspired by his bravery, but knowing the man, and the surgeon, I am certain that the surgery he performed during those 36 hours in that German tavern were his very best. He always told me that when things got tough, he focused down harder and got steadier; I know it was true in that tavern in Germany in World War II. I saw that intense focus for myself years later operating with him, and that lesson remains an inspiration to me to this day, and I draw on it directly when those times come.

As part of that behind German lines mission, I remember so vividly his description of the chest wounds he repaired. He was operating on our wounded soldiers in a German tavern converted to an emergency hospital and operating room. Normally, the chest drain tubes used to evacuate the air and blood from the wounded soldier's chest cavity after wounding or thoracic surgical repair would be placed under sterile water to prevent backflow of the air and blood being extracted from the thoracic cavity. This extraction of the intra-thoracic air and blood is essential if the wounded man is to breathe on his own, and hopefully survive. There were no modern day ventilators in that German tavern to help in this regard, nor was there even any sterile water for the chest tube drain, but . . . there was plenty of beer. So beer it was, and the chest tubes were placed into beer instead of sterile water. I loved his description of how that beer foamed so high while extracting the air from the chest cavities of our soldiers so that they could breathe on their own, and live.

When I talked to Uncle Dockie, he always related to me on a level that was both real and relevant, and I always learned something important and interesting, and often, I was inspired. His description of this mission to save wounded soldiers by operating 36 hours straight with a piece of shrapnel in his right hand in a German tavern behind enemy lines was a great example of the inspiration he provided me, and the humor, the vision of that foaming beer as it extracted that air from the chests of our wounded will be with me always. I savor that memory, and give thanks, when I pour a beer in the comfort and security of my home in a free, English speaking, USA.

Captain, My Captain:
I was born, as was my older sister Carol, several years before my Aunt Boo and Uncle Dockie had children of their own. So, little Mike and a two-years-older sister Carol had the great benefit

of an aunt and an uncle who would often entertain us for the day. In those days, my Aunt Boo was the major player in that entertainment (and the film maker too, thank goodness, some films of which still survive), because Dockie was a busy doctor. However, he was there sometimes and would always call me Burrhead in recognition of my haircut style at the time. Actually, he never quit calling me Burrhead. He could have called me most anything, Burrhead was fine with me. I liked him a lot even back then as a pup.

One of my earliest memories is of Aunt Boo taking me and sister Carol to ride the last streetcar trip from downtown Tampa to Ballast Point Park. Street cars were obsolete and this was the last run from downtown Tampa, down the center parkway of the Bayshore Boulevard, and ending at Ballast Point. It was a fun ride with her, even if the significance of the event for our city was lost on us at the time, and it remains one of my oldest and best childhood memories. Later childhood memories are all about my Uncle Dockie taking me on his boat, skiing and fishing. He was my first boating role model . . . and he was My Captain.

In my preteens, Uncle Dockie had two different boats. The first one, the *Cloe*, named after his first child, was an inboard Chris Craft runabout that he did some fishing on, but more importantly to me, he taught me to water ski with it in old Tampa Bay. I loved skiing from the beginning, and when he sold the *Cloe* to get a bigger boat, a 30 foot sport fisherman type, I hoped that I could ski behind it too. It was much bigger, and I never did ski behind it, but I did do lots of fishing with him on it, and that was even more fun than skiing.

The time of the new, big boat, the *Celeste*, was when I was about 9 – 12 years old. I remember it so well. On many Sundays, I would ask my mother to call my Uncle Dockie to see if I could go out

on his boat with him, since I knew he went out often on Sunday
afternoons to fish. Not every time that I asked her to, but often,
Mama would call Uncle Dockie and ask, "Could you use a boat
boy today?" I would stand by the phone and try to read his answer
in her face. I could usually tell the answer before she told me.

Often, the answer was, "Sure, Sadie, send Burrhead over." I'd go
over to his house, or to the marina, absolutely delighted about
my good fortune, and I always would have a great experience.
I loved them both for it at the time, but even more now. I now
know that I was a bit of a chore for my Uncle Dockie when I was
on his boat, but my mother asked him anyway and he sometimes
said yes despite that fact. The facts eventually reached me. I was
a chore because I was so inquisitive about all of the strange and
wonderful 'things' on the boat itself, and all of the miraculous
'things' he was doing to make it run and to make it do what he
wanted it to do … I wanted to understand it all and he was the
only person there to explain it to me. The fact was, I could turn
a fun, relaxing fishing trip for my uncle into a nonstop question
and answer session. Mama shared that with me one time towards
the end of that era, and I tried to do better after that, but I'm not
sure I could really, given all of the wonderful things around me
when we were fishing on his boat. A young kid's dream, and I
lived it several times a year. I remain so thankful to my Mom for
asking him and to my Uncle Dockie for saying yes and taking
me. Fabulous!

One of my favorite recollections of boating with my uncle was
the time we were trolling for Spanish Mackerel in Old Tampa
Bay. There were a number of other boats trolling that day and
everyone seemed to be doing reasonably well catching a few fish,
or so it seemed to me. I was catching a few and loving it. All of
a sudden Uncle Dockie shouted to me, "Reel'em in!" There was
no mistaking that voice; this was important. I reeled in, very

                                    My Darling Margy

quickly too. As I was doing it, Uncle Dockie raced from the aft deck to the helm, grabbed the helm and gunned both engines to what must have been full throttle. At the same time, he swung the helm over very hard, practically making a u-turn in place, and then guided the boat so that it crossed closely behind one of the boats that had been trolling the mackerel pack with us. Having crossed that other boat's stern, Uncle Dockie throttled back abruptly, still close to the boat whose stern we had just passed, and quickly returned to the stern of our boat, with a walk and posture that was both aggressive and defiant. He was obviously very mad and shouted at the other boat,

"There, how do you like a little of your own medicine, damn you!"

The captain of the other replied weakly, something, like "you ought not to do that." It was over; that was it; both boats went on fishing, and nothing more was said between the two captains. It was a very mysterious and scary event to me, and I had no idea what was going on. I didn't say a word; I just knew my captain was hot about something.

Uncle Dockie explained to me later, that the other boat he yelled at was a 'professionally captained' charter boat, that had intentionally cut off our trolling lines to prevent us from catching "their fish." I did then recall that when I reeled it in, my line had no terminal tackle on it. The other boat had stripped our tackle by intentionally cutting too close to our stern and hence cutting our lines off with their boat's propellers, to get us out of the picture so they could get more of the fish. Uncle Dockie retaliated in kind for the other captain's offense and cut off their lines, and then let that captain know exactly why he did it. Rough … but beautiful. I saw it as an honest, direct, and just response to aggression by the other captain.

It was the only time I ever saw my uncle really mad. Damn, my captain, the surgeon soldier, could take definitive action on the high seas, as well as in the operating room in Germany, and in Tampa, as I would learn 10 years later assisting him in surgery there.

Medical Inspiration and Surgical Mentor:

Having one uncle who was a doctor, another uncle who was an engineer, and a father who was an attorney imprinted me early as to how one made a living in this world. It seemed pretty simple conceptually. You went to college, and after college, you went to professional school, you studied, you trained, you got your degree, maybe you trained some more, and then you hung out your shingle. "The Doctor" or "The Lawyer" or "The Engineer" … Is In. Simple. The question was, which field to follow, which training to take, and therefore, which shingle to hang out? Until high school, I thought it was probably engineering for me since I liked to build things. My mother had always encouraged me to build, and even invent, new things. She nourished my natural inclination to build new things, and I always loved to take things apart and see how they worked and how I could improve them; or fix them if they were broken.

In my first year of high school biology, I began to see living things as the most wondrous of things that were essentially machines that really worked. How they worked was fascinating to me and the anatomy and physiology of living things was like a new level of system engineering to me. But how to be an engineer in that field? About that time, as my interest in the engineering of living things began to grow, I also discovered that my Uncle Dockie was not just a doctor, he was a SURGEON, and surgeons fixed broken living creatures using their minds, their hearts, their training, their experience, and their hands. When I asked for the details, he told me all about it, and it was exhilarating. That was it, I knew what

                                           My Darling Margy

I wanted to do. I was going to use my engineering abilities to fix people; I was going to be a surgeon like my Uncle Dockie. From that day on, I knew what I wanted to do with my life.

Over the next three years, I continued to talk to Uncle Dockie about doing surgery, and he even got me some old, but serviceable, surgical instruments, and some suture materials. He showed me how the instruments were used to make incisions, clamp bleeders, retract organs, and close the wounds. It was so fascinating, mending tissues like I could mend machines. I wanted to do it NOW! I didn't want to wait through two more years of high school, and four years of college before I could go to medical school and start learning surgery. I wanted to start surgery training right now . . . even if I had to teach myself.

One day I told Uncle Dockie that I wanted to do an exploratory abdominal laparatomy (he was already teaching me the language of surgery) on a living frog to see if I could operate on it successfully and make it survive. He didn't laugh, and indeed was very supportive of this my first surgical effort, and he got me some ether with which to anesthetize the frog. He also made a few suggestions as to how I should proceed and sent me on my way to have my first surgical experience. It was during the Christmas holidays, and I did do the exploratory lap on the anesthetized frog, and the frog did live. Seemed just fine in fact. I was so proud of my frog that I took my first patient to a family dinner gathering that Christmas Day, and there I presented my surgical triumph to Uncle Dockie for his review.

He was enthusiastic about my results and even volunteered to get more ether for my next exploratory laparotomy, which I had just announced to him would be on a laboratory rat. Turns out that the rat I bought at a pet shop had a tumor under the arm and Uncle Dockie thought was probably a breast tumor. So the exploratory laparotomy surgery plan was converted to a simple mastectomy surgery plan. I felt like I was on my way to doing real surgery, even useful surgery, since this rat had a breast tumor that really needed removal. Unfortunately the rat died during surgery, of what I interpret today as an anesthetic overdose. It was sad, but my Uncle Dockie was teaching me to be a surgeon way before medical school, and I was actually learning some surgical skills, sort of learning some anesthetic skills, and loving it all.

Continuing my surgical training through high school and college, I did many more 'operations' as a part of that early education into how to 'fix' living things, but I'd have to wait five more years before my Uncle Dockie took me into the real operating room the summer before I started medical school at his alma mater, Duke University. I was so happy to be accepted at Duke Medical School, to be going to medical school where my uncle had gone. Though my college grades were very good, Uncle Dockie wrote a letter of recommendation which I am sure helped my application. Incredibly, and I don't think these things happen very often, a person in the admissions office actually gave me Uncle Dockie's recommendation letter when I was a senior year medical student. It was wonderful and it made me know that he loved me as much as I loved him.

My first time in the human O.R. was as a second assistant to my uncle. He was on staff at Saint Joseph's Hospital, a Tampa hospital administered by Catholic nuns of the Franciscan Order. I had waited what seemed like all of my life for this moment, the moment when I would actually be participating in human surgery. I had done 6-8 surgeries on various animals with various degrees of success, but this was different, this was HUMAN surgery, and I was right there, scrubbed, gowned and gloved, and up against the table opposite my mentor in a true O.R. for the very first time. I was nervous, but oh so eager. Then, the

                    My Darling Margy

operation started, and Uncle Dockie made his opening abdominal incision through the skin. Wow! So that's how he does it. One long smooth stroke with a Number 10 Bard-Parker scalpel, and the skin incision is all done. Beautiful! That clean sharp cut through all the layers of the skin would make a beautiful scar I was thinking. He was a master, and I was watching him work.

But, wait! What's this strange feeling? All of a sudden, as the blood slowly filled the just made skin incision, and Uncle Dockie began swiftly clamping the individual bleeders, the smell of ether suddenly became overwhelming to me, and my head got light, very light. I said something to Uncle Dockie about my not feeling very good, and he chuckled softly and quickly urged in a large, very strong Sister who mercifully grabbed me under the arms and helped me back from the table to catch my breath. It was close, and her rescue came shortly before I might have fallen face forward into the wound.

Observing that opening skin incision was my total surgical experience that first day in the O.R. with my mentor. True to his fun nature, Uncle Dockie got a big kick out of it since he had warned me that despite my animal surgical experience, this was human surgery and it would feel different. However, I had assured him I was cool and not to worry about Burrhead. He got a laugh out of my quick exit that day for sure, but not as good a laugh as he, and everybody in the O.R., got on this rookie's second day in the human O.R.

Embarrassed by my surgical début, but not really daunted or discouraged, I was back scrubbed, gowned, and gloved the next morning for round two. This time the skin incision went just the same as before, the blood slowly filled the incision, and the bleeders got clamped and tied with 2-0 plain catgut (he NEVER used the electric cautery to, in his words, "Bar-B-Q a bleeder"), but this time I was his second assistant, not dizzy, and feeling great.

However, after a few minutes I began to realize that all was not well with my scrub suit, actually, my scrub suit pants to be specific. Distressingly, my scrub pants actually felt like they were FALLING OFF. Oh no, this can't be, first day I'm feeling faint, and now a problem with my scrub pants? How could this be? In those days, the O.R. scrubs were nicely pressed and even had a bit of starch in them to improve the look. Unfortunately for rookies that light starch, as I learned that second day in the O.R., could make the drawstring on the pants a little tough to cinch up tight enough to securely hold up those scrub pants, particularly when a wallet and a watch were heavy in the back pocket of those scrub pants.

I was a rookie, and a rookie has many lessons to learn. To have announced the previous day that I was light headed after a beautiful skin incision was tough enough, but now, I had to announce that my pants were falling off. Oh well, here goes, "Uncle Dockie, I think my pants are falling off." Uproarious laughter ensued at my reluctant confession, but my favorite Big Sister came to my rescue. It was a different rescue from day one, but she knew the drill. She firmly grabbed the waist band of my scrub pants, now around my ankles, and pushed my pants back up, under my gown, roughly to my waist, and secured them with a towel clamp through the back of my gown and through the back of my now properly positioned pants.

Thank you Sister for being so skillful and not including my skin in that towel clamp rig you constructed to deal with this O.R. emergency and that held up my pants so well for the next 3 hours. All of the surgical crew, particularly my Uncle Dockie, were still chuckling at the end of the case. Much to his delight, ole

					My Darling Margy

Burrhead had entertained them again.

After those two faux pas, I never had any problem in the O.R. associated with my head or my pants. I subsequently scrubbed with Uncle Dockie dozens of times, and with his training, I became reasonably skilled for a medical student learning to be a surgeon. Uncle Dockie had great hands. He could cut or tie one handed, with either hand, and he taught me to do it too. I practiced until I was very good at it, and he let me do more and more when I assisted him. He would even ask me to come in and be his assistant when I was in town, and that made me feel great. I studied and emulated his moves constantly, so when I assisted him, I usually knew what was coming next, and I was generally right there with him.

When I was a junior in medical school, I had a surgical rotation at Watts Hospital in Durham. One day, I was assisting a surgeon there on a case who was allowing me to do much of the ligatures and tying of bleeders. I always liked that and appreciated the surgeons that allowed me to do something other than hold a retractor. I was good, really by any standards, at tying and was proficiently tying off each bleeder. The surgeon commented, "You tie well; where did you learn to tie like that?" Even though I knew he would have no idea who I was crediting with my tying skills, I simply said. "My uncle, who is a surgeon in Tampa taught me to tie." His next question was, "Who is your uncle?" "Frank Chunn", was my answer. To my shock, he replied with out any hesitation, "You had a very good teacher. I know Frank Chunn; I was in school with him. Great surgeon." Small world.

As it turned out, the surgical skills that I learned from my Uncle Dockie, and lots of dry practice at my surgery practice station, actually helped me get into what ended up being my ultimate medical career. At the time I was a medical student at Duke, the biomedical engineering department there was very new and was fortunately very cross disciplinary in that both engineering and medical faculty were championing and managing the new graduate program in BME. As a part of our junior year curriculum in medical school, we had a course called "Emergency War Surgery" in which we would do laceration repairs and tracheostomies on anesthetized dogs as a training for major military or civil emergencies.

That stuff was old hat to me by that time, but still fun and I did it well and enjoyed it. However, I was wanting bigger things. I had managed to get a short piece of Dacron aortic graft that I was just dying to see if I could implant in a dog. The dogs were there, they were anesthetized, the class was officially over, and this was my chance. So after the official Emergency War Surgery lab was over, I recruited a couple of adventurous fellow students to assist me as I attempted to remove a section of dog's healthy abdominal aorta and replace it with that small piece of Dacron graft.

I had seen the aortic graft procedure in the O.R. observation room several times and I thought I could do it. It would be better if we had the proper tools, but let's try anyway. All we had to work with were some Kelly clamps, a few Hallsteads, a needle holder, a few retractors, a pair of scissors, and a scalpel. We started the "case" enthusiastically, but not surprisingly, there turned out to be a fair amount of uncharted terrain for this "see one, do one" budding surgeon. But we muddled through it, and the dog survived. One of the senior instructors, a man I did not know at the time, watched our efforts fairly attentively that late afternoon. He nodded approval at our success, but he really didn't say anything to us. And he never introduced himself.

That aortic graft procedure was a fun experience, and it worked. But, my next week's after class surgery case was an attempt to do a kidney transplant from one dog to another. It didn't work; the vessels were too small, the tools too crude, and my skills too thin. C'est la vie, I was practicing my skills; next time it will be better.

At the time of that makeshift, but successful, graft procedure, I didn't know that the observer was a well known academic surgeon at Duke, Dr. Smith. I eventually met him for the first time the next year when I interviewed for the National Institute of Health's Biomedical Engineering graduate school fellowship for which I had applied. It was the same Dr. Smith who had nodded his approval the previous year who turned out to be my medical school interviewer for the NIH fellowship. He had important input regarding the selection of the recipient of the award that I was hoping to win. Dr. Smith and I had a good talk about my goal of being both a surgeon and a biomedical engineer, and I emphasized that getting a grant for graduate work towards a PhD in BME would be my first choice for my next career training phase.

He seemed supportive of my plans, and encouraged me to continue to find a way to combine those two fields, engineering and surgery. At the end of the interview, he let me know that he had actually seen some of my early surgical efforts the previous year, and that he was surprised at what he had seen, and impressed. Very strange . . .the surgical skills taught to me in large part by my uncle in Tampa, help me win a fellowship for engineering graduate school at Duke that ultimately changes my career path away from surgery into biomedical engineering.

Uncle Dockie never knew that story, I never told him; but I should have. I know he would have loved it, that his Burrhead, as a junior in medical school and using techniques that he had taught me, did some animal surgery just for fun that helped him get a five year scholarship for a PhD in BME. That fellowship, and the training in BME that resulted, ultimately changed my career path to engineering, but I know Uncle Dockie would have been proud of me, even if he was also a little disappointed that I would not be a surgeon.

For the first three years of my PhD work, I still fully intended to go back into surgery after I finished the PhD. I continued to build my surgery skills at Duke in the lab, and when I was back in Tampa, I would assist my uncle in the OR most every day. Over the six years following those first two humiliating OR episodes, I had gotten pretty good for a surgical rookie, and I always thought Uncle Dockie liked my style. After all, though not polished, my style was really his style. For sure, my style was not fully formed, not mature, and I was not smooth and sure like he was. But my surgery style, both mentally and technically, which was patterned so much after his style, showed promise, and I was still striving for his confidence and excellence even while in graduate school. I always believed, and cherished the notion, that when I finished my PhD and my formal surgical training, that my uncle, who was always my inspiration, my mentor, and my idol, would let me come back to Tampa and go into practice with him. C. Frank Chunn, MD, and Maynard Ramsey III, MD, Partners in the Practice of Surgery. That's what I wanted; I knew I could do it; only about 8 more years of training to go.

I Miss You Uncle Dockie:
It was about 7:30 PM when I learned that my Uncle Dockie had died. I was 27 years old at the time, and I remember the phone call from my mother that night, telling me Uncle Dockie had a heart attack while tending his boat at the Tampa Yacht Club and that he had died there. I was married, living in Durham after completing medical school a year earlier, and I was working towards a PhD in Biomedical Engineering. I was all alone that night because my wife, Lynn, was on a botany field trip on the

My Darling Margy

Eastern Shore of North Carolina as a part of her National Science Foundation scholarship course at Duke that summer. That call rocked my world like nothing ever had; it was so unexpected, so tragic, and damn it, so sad.

I called the airlines for a flight to Tampa the next morning. I left my wife a note saying that Dockie had died, that I had gone to Tampa for his funeral, that I would be back after it was over, and that I just had to go without waiting for her to return. I left the next morning on a very sad journey, leaving my note and our two cats to meet her. In those days, long distance telephone calls were tougher to make, even if you knew the number; and there were no cell phones. So, Lynn had to learn the sad news from my note later that day when she returned to Durham. Uncle Dockie was a good friend of hers too.

On my sad trip home to Tampa that morning, I reflected on all the good days I had spent assisting my Uncle Dockie in the OR when I was in Tampa on vacations from medical and graduate school. And I reflected on our time in the doctor's lounge between cases when usually, I would sit close by and listen to him as he dictated his operative notes on the phone after each case, and I tried to mentally hone my own imitation of those OP notes, knowing that I would be dictating them in the future after my cases. He would dictate, I would listen, and often, he would smoke a Chesterfield cigarette. After dictating, he would talk to me as he smoked that cigarette, and he always told me, shaking the cigarette in his hand at me, "Don't you ever start this. It's almost impossible to stop once you start it. And it'll kill you." I knew he meant it and I never started.

When I got the call that night in Durham, I was sick … I had lost my uncle, my surgeon mentor, and my good friend. A man who had been a major influence and role model in my life. I was

27 then, and by that time in my life, I thought I was pretty much fully formed both as a person and as a physician-engineer; at least it seemed that way to me then. Fully formed at 27? I think so, but I don't know really. But I do know that I am so lucky that I had my Uncle Dockie for 27 years, and that I am still so grateful that it was for the first 27 years of my life, during those formative years where he made so much difference for me.

In my life I have had a number of major influences, all of whom I am so appreciative of, and all of whom have made some positive difference in my life. The three persons to whom I'm most indebted though are my mother Sarah Moore Ramsey, my father Maynard Ramsey, Jr., and my uncle, Charles Frank Chunn . . . always my Uncle Dockie.

It has been 35 years since he left us, and yet I still feel his presence in my life every day.
And I still miss him . . . a lot.

Editor's Note: Dr. Mike Ramsey is the developer of the DINAMAP, "the first automated, noninvasive oscillometric device to measure blood pressure and the first medical monitor to use a microprocessor." He holds over 29 U.S. patents as well as additional international patents. He is the recipient of the 2005 Association for the Advancement of Medical Instrumentation (AAMI) Foundation Laufman/Greatbatch Prize. [1]

[1] http://www.aami.org/publications/AAMINews/2005may/0505.awards.html

Acknowledgements

Thanks to all who have encouraged us to get this book completed. There are many friends and family members and we are grateful for the support and encouragement in all the forms it was given. Special thanks to Martin Baron; Dr. Alston Callahan; Cloe Chunn; Dudley Clendinen; Kevin Francis Colcord; Kevin Thomas Colcord; Ann Fox, PhD; The Honorable Sam Gibbons; The Reverend Jim Harnish; Leonard Levy; Gary Mormino; PhD; Ann Murphey; David Murphey; Wanda Mukherjee; Mike Ramsey; Mary Semans; Lamar Sparkman; and Trisha White, MD.